Chairman Biden and Dr. Fauci's Monster

Revised Edition

Ronald Alfred Weitzman

To my wife, Morley, and my daughter Leora and in memory of my daughter Karen

ABOUT THE AUTHOR

For the author of this book, Ron Weitzman, education made a gigantic difference in his family. Born outside the United States, Ron's father barely made it through the third grade here. Thanks to America's equality of opportunity, Ron worked his way with the help of scholarships and fellowships to a BA and MA from Stanford and a PhD from Princeton. He has received a Stanford Honors Fellowship; Psychometric Fellowship of Princeton and the Educational Testing Service; and two post-doctoral fellowships, from the National Science Foundation and the United States Public Health Service.

Ron has served on university faculties in the United States, the United Kingdom, and Israel. His specialty areas are mental tests and survey statistics, and he has dozens of publications and three patents in those fields (one in the first and two in the second).

Though Ron is in his ninety-fourth year, this is his first book. Until now, working solely within his fields of expertise and within the communities where he has made his home, he has lived his life according to

Voltaire's famous advice: "One must cultivate one's own garden." What Voltaire feared—the triumph of the worst of mankind, which is what our country is facing now—has changed Ron's mind. He hopes that this book will change yours in the same direction, toward action, including voting, to help restore America the beautiful.

PREFACE

This book has two purposes: The first is to destroy the negative and inaccurate stereotype of voters who support Donald Trump held by most Democrats, about half of Independents, and over one-third of Republicans. The second, in the process of carrying out the first, is to shed light on important aspects of troubling national issues, aspects that most of the media have left in the dark. The importance of those aspects is that their inclusion in our understanding of the issues may help us resolve them. The chapter titles identify the issues. My writing is informal. I hope you will enjoy it.

TABLE OF CONTENTS

CHAPTER 1

Left, Right, March

OJ, can't you see by the dim candlelight

Whom so fiercely you slew with your single-edged saber.

Whose broad swipes and deep thrusts through the perilous

fight Cast the blood that you shed as a sign of your labor?

But why not a gun, and why did you run?

If you did not do it, then who was the one?

Or do those ill-fitting gloves point a finger of blame

At a black-burning Mark in a blood-spattered frame?

The liberal center of Franklin Delano Roosevelt is dead, finally, after years of battle between the Right and the Left in American politics. Rather than killing each other, the two sides succeeded only in destroying their common ground. Even Vice President Kamala Harris, as an evangelical proponent of Venn diagrams, can see that.

That common ground was a truce between the two sides, allowing a caretaker government to coexist with free-enterprise capitalism. Such coexistence has always been unstable from its very beginning in the French Revolution.

During the Storming of the Bastille, the French Assembly met to form a new government, a republic, with members supporting veto power for the king seated on the right side of the assembly leader and members supporting zero power for the king seated on the left side. Since then, conservatives, who support limited change, have been considered right-wing and progressives, who support radical change, left-wing.

France has suffered the instability of Left-Right government in the many rebirths of its republic, now in its fifth incarnation. Other countries have not fared so well. Killing its tzar, Russia veered leftward, with the inevitable replacement of the tzar by a dictator. Germany did likewise, its left-leaning national socialist government also ending up in a dictatorship. Although a common belief is that right-wing governments end up in dictatorship, history demonstrates the opposite: The road to the Left, not to the Right, ends in dictatorship. That, in fact, is the direction our government in America is now headed, with President Biden every day looking more and more like Chairman Xi of the Chinese dictatorship—a revelation that has now become transparently clear in the Biden government's serial prosecutions of Donald Trump, Biden's most threatening rival in the 2024 election.

How did the United States until recently fare better than other countries in enduring the tension between Left and Right? The answer is that the United States uniquely in its founding documents replaced the King of England with God. Our currency and our Pledge of Allegiance remind us every day that God is our King. The fourth verse of "America," ironically sung to the tune of "God Save the King," leaves no doubt about it:

Our Father, God, to Thee,

Author of Liberty,

To Thee we sing.

Long may our land be bright

With Freedom's holy light.

Protect us by Thy might,

Great God, our King.

During the nineteenth century, as our country grew from East to West and as immigrants from all over the world assimilated in the great growing together of *e pluribus unum*, the Bible served as our manual of coexistence, most explicitly in the West.

So what has happened since then?

The American Left, which, at best, had only tolerated God, now has exhausted not only that particular tolerance but also, exhaustively, tolerance itself. The progressive wing of the Democratic Party is leading our country away from God and freedom, both economic and otherwise, toward rigid government rule in the form of a Marxist "dictatorship of the proletariat." Though *of* the people (proletariat), that dictatorship is not *by* the people. Rather, it is by a self-appointed elite who has been consolidating its power via any means possible, including censorship and thought control, under a bought and paid-for puppet administration. Recent books by Mark R. Levin provide the whole history.

Here, the focus will be on the Biden administration, how it came into power and what it is doing to take God out of government and convert the United States into a China of the West.

During his four decades in the House and Senate and eight years as vice president, Joseph Robinette Biden Jr. did not originate much legislation, but rising from train commuter to jet-setter, he did make a lot of money. Just how he did that is now under investigation in Congress. How he became the Democrats' nominee needs no investigation.

Just plain common sense can give us the answer. Biden was trailing near the rear in the intraparty debates and, more importantly, in the early voting states of Iowa and New Hampshire. Then, miracle of miracles, he triumphed in the next state (South Carolina) election and, from then on, was a shoo-in. Why? His sole, true intraparty competitor following South Carolina was Bernie Sanders, popular among Democrats but a no-no for the coming interparty election because he was so far to the Left, not merely an admitted but, even more notably, a proud socialist. So, in Biden Speak, here was the deal: Sanders, together with his powerful fellow travelers on the Left, would support Biden if Biden would support their Leftist agenda. The fix was in, and so was Biden. The reason was not that he was so good at campaigning—with time spent mostly in his basement—but that the far-Left wing of his party was so good at getting out the vote.

From the standpoint of his opponent, Donald Trump, maybe that word "good" on the last line of the preceding paragraph should, as here, be separated from the rest of the previous sentence by quotation marks. For Trump and many of his supporters, the means used by hardcore Democrats to win not only the nomination but also the election for Biden were anything but good, at least insofar as good means proper, fair, or legal. The rest of that story is for a later chapter. Nor is the story here how the Biden administration is leading our capitalistic republic under God down the path to godless, socialist one-party rule or—in a single word—dictatorship. That is a story we are all living now.

The story here is about how Democrats and Republicans got their party affiliations. Most partisan voters, we can agree, got their party affiliation from their parents. For those people, their party is not merely an affiliation; it is their identification. As such, it is hard to change. If party is a family identification resistant to change, then a fair question to ask is how the family got that identification. The Civil War is a good part of the explanation. Unlike people in the North, people in the South tended to be Democrats. To rebuild following their loss in that war, Democrats increasingly relied on immigration as the way to do it. Because of their need for help in the process of assimilation, immigrants, especially from non-English-speaking countries, have been drawn to that—what had become a—caretaker party.

Here is an example from my personal experience: When I was five years old in early 1936, a large panel truck rumbling down the street came to a stop in front of the apartment building where I lived with my mother and two younger brothers in a Jewish immigrant neighborhood on the southside of Chicago. When I looked out the window, I saw that the truck's occupants were handing out to each adult not only a crisp, new five-dollar bill but also a framed portrait of Franklin Deleno Rosevelt so large it was as tall as I was. I knew that because, like dozens of our neighbors, my mother and I rushed down from our third-floor apartment to get our freebies. Five dollars was a lot of money during the Depression, which was at its peak that winter early in the voting season. The Democrats were working not only early but also hard in our immigrant community to ensure the election of Roosevelt to his second term.

What about Republicans, who did not benefit from the boost of immigration following the Civil War? A notable difference between Right and Left is that voters on the Left tend to live in large cities while voters on the Right tend to live in small towns or rural areas. Consideration of the reason for that is important if only for electioneering purposes. Large cities are large largely because immigrants from around the world settled there in large numbers within neighborhoods where people speaking a common language other than English needed help from a caretaker party in their process of assimilation. As noted earlier, that caretaker party, at least since the Civil War, has been the one on the Left. Meanwhile, many people who were fluent in English or otherwise needed no caretaker- party help took the opportunity of an opening West to resettle there, many as families, in their own businesses on their own properties, without government intervention except for the protection of property rights. The party on the Right was naturally and traditionally the party for them.

Primarily because of immigration, Democrats outnumbered Republicans from the time of Democrat Woodrow Wilson to the time of Democrat Lyndon Johnson, when his legislation that removed racial restraints on voting turned the tide. The formerly Solid South Democrats, who had suppressed the Black vote, suddenly turned into Solid South Republicans.

Currently, the two parties are now approximately evenly matched, accounting for about 23 percent of registered voters each.

Counting party membership, as well as how it came to be, is important, but even more important, at least for electioneering, are the ideologies that distinguish the two parties. Although people do not often change their ideologies, the ideologies themselves tend to evolve.

An ideology is a belief system that governs behavior. Ideologies are convenient and practical because people do not usually have time to examine every decision they make independently. Though differing, most ideologies are moral to the extent that they support human life and well-being.

What differentiates the ideologies on the Left and on the Right today is that the Left seeks equity of outcome, and the Right seeks equality of opportunity. The Left focuses on the destination, good or bad, and the Right focuses on the journey, right way or wrong way. Both views are moral, but the first without the second is not.

The prophet Micah prayed, "Let justice flow down as waters, and Righteousness as a mighty stream." Because the scales of justice hang equally low, some people may interpret the first clause to be a prayer for equity of outcome, and it is, but only in the punishment of incorrect behavior. The second clause is clearly a prayer for correct behavior. Of course, for the behavior to be good, as well as correct, the goals should also be worthy. So the obvious general moral here is that we must all do what is both good and right. Politically, that means to survive and thrive in this world, our country needs both Democrats on the Left and Republicans on the Right working together toward consensus. Unfortunately, now that ship of state is foundering.

Fundamentally, the two parties differ in their answers to the question, What is the appropriate application of equity of outcome? According to Democrats today, equity applies to outcomes of all behavior except misbehavior. That, however, is precisely the opposite of its traditional application, which is solely to the punishment of crimes. Justice must be equitable. Prosecutors must administer punishments equal to crimes regardless of who commits them. Traditionally, equity has applied to outcomes solely of misbehavior, not of all other behavior, for which in every contest, the outcome would be equal for everyone. Of the two parties today, only Republicans seem to hold to that tradition.

Today's Democrats have turned the traditional reward-punishment system upside down. Equity, to them, no longer applies to justice. Prosecutors now charge Republicans and Democrats inequitably for the same questionable behavior by identifying it as misbehavior solely for Republicans. The glaringly different prosecutorial treatment of Democrats Hillary Clinton and Joseph Biden on one side of the political aisle and Republican Donald Trump on the other for their questionable handling of classified data is starkly clear evidence of that.

The Hebrew word for an adversary is "Satan" (pronounced in Hebrew as SA-TUN). When used in the Bible as the adversary of God, English translators interpreted that word as the Devil. The Bible itself also identifies Satan as the prosecutor in the court of God.

That, prophetically, is what a prosecutor has today become for Democrats, an avatar of the Devil, in whose mind and practice, good and bad have reversed roles. Victims have no justice as prosecutors let perpetrators go free, with no bail or jail time. Why? In the minds of the prosecutors who do that, there being only so much wealth in the world, victims must have oppressed their perpetrators by taking the perpetrators' share of that wealth from them. How could a prosecutor, having that mindset, intensify the oppression by punishing the perpetrator? The mindset in that question is uniquely the mindset of a Marxist. Rather than equity of outcome, however, justice is equity of crime and punishment. Justice today for Democrats is not only inequitable but it is also upside down on the moral compass.

When in 2020 Democrats seized power, earned or otherwise, the power, filling their heads, left no room for judgment or common sense. Immediately, without a pause for thought, Biden reversed every consequential regulation of his predecessor. His administration's behavior has been like the behavior of adolescents no longer restrained by their parents. What was bad is now good. Homosexuality was bad, punished severely in the Bible; now it is good, celebrated each year in America by Gay Pride Month.

Closed borders were good, but not now. Likewise is the story for cheap and available energy from the ground, now dumped in favor of its opposite, costly and insufficient energy from the sky (sun and wind)—upside down or backwards, like almost everything else in life under the Biden administration today, including the cost of living and the give-and-take of foreign relations.

The Biden administration aside for a moment, a fair question to consider is what differences in overall mindset might distinguish members of the two major American political parties. Republicans certainly can claim patriotism as its dominant political mindset. Though not eschewing patriotism entirely, Democrats are basically romanticists. Rather than Ronald Reagan, Robin Hood is their romantic hero: Steal from (tax) the rich to help the poor. That leads to the equity sought by Democrats. Contrariwise, Republicans, with patriotic fervor, believe in law and order and a strong military protecting property and assuring equality of opportunity for everyone, both rich and poor. That contrast is obvious in the vast difference in life under Trump and Biden, with the extremities under Biden now threatening the very existence of our country.

To understand how that is happening, a brief look at the Kibbutz Movement in Israel might help. Kibbutzim are the essential embodiment of a centralized government democratically assuring that the distribution of goods and services occurs according to the Marxian dictum "from each according to his ability, to each according to his need." (Today's Democrats may feel uncomfortable with that dictum, not for what it says but for how it says it. Though bastardizing the English language, they would replace the singular pronoun "his" by the plural pronoun "their" for the sake of equity.)

The Kibbutz Movement in Israel began in 1909 when a relatively small number of Jews, mostly from Eastern Europe, settled in Palestine in an early effort of the Zionist movement to bring Jews back from the diaspora to their Holy Land home from which the Romans had expelled them in AD 70. The settlement was on barren land, which the settlers had no experience to till, but the goal was to transform it so that, as foretold in the Old Testament, the "desert would bloom like the rose," a romantic goal if there ever was one.

The settlers organized a government that was truly democratic and equitable, no one needing or using money, which, along with the entire settlement, belonged to the whole group. The entire adult membership participated equally in decision-making discussions led by a work organizer, a treasurer, and a secretary, who was the effective leader of the kibbutz. Every adult was available to do every job that needed to be done, except for the infirm or the elderly, whom the kibbutz supported, along with the children. All children in the early kibbutzim were separated not only by age but also from their parents, with adult caregivers assigned to each age group as nurses for the very young and as teachers or counselors for the rest. From the single group of 1909 settlers, kibbutzim grew to about 270 today, which constitute about 2.5 percent of the Israeli population. With their growth in number, the kibbutzim also evolved in their social structure. The top three positions are now full-time jobs. Except perhaps for infants, children now are no longer reared in age groups, separated from their parents, but are brought up by their families until they reach high school age. That change, together with the small kibbutz percentage of the population, shows the limits of socialized governments that have not devolved into dictatorships. Few kibbutzim have been larger than one thousand members.

The government of Israel, though rising from socialized structures, today exists as a vibrant capitalistic, powerful, and innovative democracy, a status no kibbutz, with all members constrained to be socially and economically equal, could ever achieve. Different from Israel, the United States, under Biden, has chosen in fanciful illusion to devolve leftward toward dictatorship in one-party rule rather than remain a two-party capitalistic republic in pursuit of equality of opportunity rather than equity of outcome.

In this process, politics in America has become a blood sport, a comparison that requires attention. Voters identify with political parties with the same intensity that fans identify with sports teams. Both have a common goal: to win. The two differ, however, in the regulation of their games. Sports have rules enforced by referees. Politics has no rules and no referees, a situation that has motivated the Biden administration in its pursuit of one-party rule to use the third branch of our government to prosecute opponents under laws that do not exist. No law makes it illegal to question the validity of an election, but Democrats are now prosecuting Donald Trump and his supporters for doing just that. The United States is no longer Ronald Reagan's shining city on the hill. By political wind and fire, that city has gone the way of Lahaina on Maui.

What makes sports work is competition, which, when conducted properly, also makes politics work. In fact, from the time of Charles Darwin, we have known that competition is what makes life itself work. So we should also know that competition is what makes an economy work. That is a lesson that too many Democrats in the United States seem to have forgotten if they have ever learned it. Sports are a true metaphor for politics, and the measure of our love of the one and hatred of the other is the extent to which fair competition plays a role in each.

The attempt of the Left to suppress the role of competition not only in politics but also in our schools and even in our workplaces, if unchecked, will end in the death of our country. The goal of the Right today is not just to Make America Great Again; it is to save our very lives. The pursuit of equity is the pursuit of stagnation. Equality of opportunity is the sole mechanism of innovation and life-saving change. This is not an optional religion; it is a fact of life. To right our foundering ship of state, we must tilt it rightward. Doing that requires that more than half of us move our weight to the Right. That is what we must do with our vote in the presidential election of 2024.

Some Democrats are so extreme in their pursuit of equity that they want to get rid of testing in school to avoid hurting students' feelings. To do that, teaching without testing, would be like playing football without keeping score. Should we do that to avoid hurting the feelings of the losing team? Are the feelings of poorly performing students more important than the feelings of a poorly performing team? The Biden administration's leap to the Left has opened a Pandora's box of romantic but mindlessly irresponsible changes.

Both the Left and Right parties have evolved since their inception while retaining their fundamental differences, the Right's concern with the income and the Left's with the outflow of governmental money. Each party has moderated the evolutionary trend of the other until now. Since 2020, with the advent of the Biden administration, Democrats have burst out of the traditional two-party commons and run wild in their party's lurch leftward.

With a president and both legislative chambers under their control during their first two years in office, far Left Democrats traveled a long way in their march on the path of socialism toward the single- party rule of atheistic communist dictatorship. In preparation for this movement, they have, for years, groomed young people in schools and colleges to be their foot soldiers by exploiting the ideological vulnerability of adolescence. Democrats have excited the vulnerable with new causes like saving the world from global warming and atoning for the mistreatment of people who differ from the norm in causes that are so critical that their pursuit requires breaking traditional norms, even to the extent of turning them upside down. Censorship replaces freedom of speech. Persecution of enemies replaces prosecution of crimes. What had been good has now become evil, and what had been evil has now become good, as noted earlier. This vision of a new world has been engraved in the minds of people who have been assuming leadership roles in business, government, and the arts and sciences.

Just as the foot soldiers have been tumbling traditional statues and defacing traditional art, the government has perverted the conduct and reporting of scientific studies to strengthen its power, most notably with respect to the pandemic and global warming. Following the death of George Floyd, hundreds of "good" mobs, for months, destroyed businesses, killed cops, and burned police stations for all of which no one was prosecuted while a single "bad" mob stormed the Capitol in protest of the 2020 presidential election with an entirely different outcome. During its two hours there without guns or torches, this "bad" mob suffered the shooting death of one of its members at the hands of an unidentified and unprosecuted police officer and, afterward, the prosecutions of almost all the others, some receiving long jail sentences. The treatments of Trump and Biden by our American "justice" systems are so blatant in their disparity that they require further examination in later chapters.

Justice in the United States no longer flows down as waters. The government has dammed it, and that is damnable. In the process of that reprehensible achievement, Democrats have interchanged the *G* of *God* and the *g* of *government.*

Just as God helps those who help themselves, so government must help the others. In their appeals for votes, Republicans focus on the first group and Democrats on the second. That explains why Democrats want to keep the Southern border open to immigrants who need all the help from government they can get. When they fail to vote, members of the first group do so because they are busy and members of the second because they are lazy. That is why Republicans want to make election day a national holiday, and Democrats want to extend the election period for as many days as possible. Democrats' success in doing that during the pandemic was a major reason they won the presidency in 2020.

Readers wondering what the lyrics about the OJ Simpson trial at the beginning of this chapter might have to do with its subject of Left versus Right in American politics need wonder no longer. Those who recognize the tune to which the lyrics are to be sung as the American National Anthem are indeed correct. Those who condemn the lyrics as such are also correct. (Admission: After the trial was over, realizing they were naughty, I could not help writing those lyrics, which I planned to share only with my wife.) Anyone who sings those lyrics to that tune is contemptible—except perhaps to current-day Democrats. And that is part of the reason they are posted there. The other part is that much of what has changed in the party on the Left has taken place since the time of that trial. To the extent that is true, an obvious question to ask is whether that trial might have had any role in producing the change.

Different from now, the bad guy then was Black, and even before the trial, most White people believed OJ was guilty. What is more, the trial did not change their minds; most, even after he was acquitted by a jury of his peers, still believed he was guilty. What has changed since then is not that belief but the willingness to share it.

At a party of Black and White people shortly after the trial, I was the only White person who openly agreed with the jury, and only one Black person had the courage to agree with me publicly. He was Famous Wade, sorrowfully dead now. We believed the missing blood in the vial taken from OJ was the source of the drops or swipes of blood found on the floor in his house or on his white Bronco. The gloves did not fit. Those were the main points of our argument, which we made fervently. Other people at the party who agreed with us were reluctant to speak out perhaps because of the unpopularity of our view at the time, particularly among White people, or perhaps because of a simple desire to avoid participation in an argument, especially at a social gathering. How that has all changed! Even White people who disagreed with us then might speak on our side now, the other side having lost its popularity, and Black people other than the exceptional Famous Wade might now equally express their views. Today, an attorney like Johnnie Cochran might even convince an all-white jury that, shoe size being about right, the White Kato Kaelin rather than the Black OJ had committed the horrendous crime.

Since that trial in 1995, Democrats have thrown an increasingly dark pale on the progress of our country toward a more perfect union, the plethora of virtue-signaling gestures made by them notwithstanding.

CHAPTER 2

Abortion

Abortion: **A Matter of Religion Rather than Government**

Then the Lord God formed the man of dust from the ground and breathed into his nostrils the breath of life, and the man became a living creature.

—Genesis 2:7

Effraenatam: No restraint

For many people, as the previous chapter observed, identification with a political party is like identification with a sports team, both being hard to change. Omitted there was religious identification, which is likely even harder to change for many people because of its existence for generations within their families. The omission was intentional because religion is so controversial that any casual reference to it might create an unnecessary diversion or distraction. In this chapter, that possibility cannot be avoided. Indeed, in this chapter, religion is at the very core of its subject, which, as the chapter's title indicates, is abortion.

Abortion itself, of course, is also controversial, but that is largely because of its very intertwinement with religion. The controversy involving that intertwinement has never been subdued, but recently, it has exploded in response to the Supreme Court's decision to reverse the 1973 *Roe v. Wade* affirmation of a constitutional right to abortion. According to the court's reversal opinion, written by Justice Samuel Alito, the Constitution does not confer the right to abortion, even implicitly, as argued in *Roe v. Wade* and subsequently by the court prior to the current ruling. The basis of the current ruling is that the regulation of abortion is subject to the Tenth Amendment to the Constitution—the so-called states-rights amendment—according to which, "[t]he powers not delegated to the United States by the Constitution, nor prohibited by it to the states, are reserved to the states respectively, or to the people."

The Constitution was carefully written, and its interpretation should be no less careful. That has not always been the case, especially when careful interpretation could lead to an undesired outcome. That, indeed, is the case with the reversal of *Roe v. Wade*.

Many members of the House and Senate believe they can enact a federal law either forbidding abortion or enabling it under some or no conditions. Neither is true. The Tenth Amendment, read carefully, explicitly (though conditionally) relegates that power solely to the states.

Other than Trump, Republicans seeking their party's nomination for the presidency also have not read the Constitution carefully. In their first televised debate on August 23, 2023, they argued about the extent to which Congress might restrict abortion but not about whether it, in fact, had the power to restrict it to any or no extent. The Tenth Amendment does not give them that power; it gives it only to the states, so long as nothing else in the Constitution forbids even that. Eight Republicans, seeking their party's nomination, stood on a national stage and demonstrated to the entire nation on television that they were all Constitutionally illiterate. What a disappointment!

Republicans aren't the only ones who have trouble reading the Constitution. Democrats are no better at that.

Congressional members of both parties believe they can enact legislation affecting abortion. The only difference between them is the extent to which they would affect it. Republicans, as a party, seek to eliminate it entirely. Democrats, as a party, seek no restrictions whatever on abortion, leaving the choice to do it exclusively to pregnant women. As noted earlier, Republicans on the debate stage abandoned their party's dominant view of total elimination of abortion in favor of its restriction to the early months of pregnancy. That moderation is due less to personal belief than to expediency. Because voters nationally are in the middle of the two extreme positions, seekers of the presidency must openly support a moderate position if they truly expect to win a national election.

Just what is that belief that motivates most Republicans and why do most Democrats seem not to share it? Many Republicans are observant Catholics, and the Catholic Church forbids abortion. Most other Republicans are members of Christian denominations that separated from the Catholic Church during the Protestant Reformation, which began in 1517, shortly before the Catholic Church first banned abortions. That occurred in 1588 when Pope Sixtus V issued a papal bull, called the E*ffraenatam* (without restraint), officially classifying abortion at any stage of fetal development as homicide, exposing anyone who commits it to excommunication and worldly punishment. Before that date, Catholics had distinguished between an animated and an unanimated fetus and banned abortions only prior to animation despite dispute about precisely when that occurs during pregnancy. Protestants, to this day, hold on to that earlier Catholic belief, including the dispute over just when animation begins.

Although many Christian Democrats are Protestants, why do they, as a party, support abortion at all stages of pregnancy? A likely reason is that few of them are truly observant Christians who are aware of any relationship between abortion and religion. Decline in religious observance and identification is a recent phenomenon, which has been growing at an increasing rate in the past quarter century. According to the Pew Research Center, Christians who outnumbered atheists or agnostics by five to one in 2007 now outnumber them by only two to one. This so-called secularization of America should come as no surprise to observers of the country's partisan politics, especially since about 2008.

That was the year prior to the Obama administration, during which the country began to emulate European socialism. Socialism is the siren song of communism, and the path of socialism leads to agnosticism, if not Marxist atheism. Tragically, for America, the fellow travelers along that path have been accelerating their pace under Biden. Neither abortion on demand nor the pace of its increasing popularity by themselves constitute that tragedy, however. Their coupling with secularization on the march to communism is what makes them tragic. In the following examination of the issue of just when the animation of a fetus occurs, this chapter will substantiate that conclusion.

Psychologists distinguish between sensation and perception. The first involves only the autonomic nervous system, which responds reflexively to events inside and outside the body without cognitive awareness. Involving the somatic nervous system, the second does require cognitive awareness to adapt to the environment. An example might clarify the difference:

Princeton University used to have shacks behind its football stadium where professors, graduate students, and research assistants did psychological research on animals. When I, as a graduate student, was doing research in one of those shacks, a research assistant was doing hers in a nearby one-room shack. I was curious about her research because it was noisy. When I asked her what she was doing, she invited me to come see it. This was what I saw. I saw a young woman wielding a mallet almost as long as she was tall. She had a huge turtle on the floor in front of her, and after electronically creating a sound having a specific pitch and loudness and swinging the mallet with great vigor, she struck the turtle on its head, which, of course, it immediately and reflexively withdrew. She kept repeating that sound and striking the turtle on the head until, following the sound, the turtle withdrew its head before she could strike it. After that occurred, she lowered the loudness or raised the pitch a notch until the turtle no longer withdrew its head immediately following the sound. In this way, she mapped the pitch and loudness ranges of the turtle's sensitivity to sound. The turtle's response to the sounds was a mindless reflex involving its autonomic nervous system. Sensation was the subject of the study. It might have been perception if the turtle had withdrawn its head immediately after the research assistant entered the room.

The following remark is entirely unnecessary, but I cannot resist making it: Now, after reading this story, no one can claim that going to Princeton is not going to a school of hard knocks.

The distinction between sensation and perception is important for the determination of the time during pregnancy when animation of the fetus occurs. Some people believe it is when the fetus first moves in response to an environmental stimulus, like a sound. That would be a matter of sensation, not perception. Perception requires mental identification, most commonly visual or auditory, of objects or sounds in a changing environment. Responses to perceptions are intentional rather than reflex. Perceptions and responses to them, as observed earlier, require cognition. Simply a response to a change in the environment is not evidence of that. So if the advent of cognition is the beginning of animation, no movement of a fetus by itself can be indicative of that.

Does cognition make a difference? When a person has an illness or an accident that causes brain death, the law allows ending the physical existence of the person without punishment, in the belief that death has already occurred. On the other side of life, the Bible treats a fetus prior to birth in the same way, not already dead but not yet alive. According to the Bible, Genesis 2–7, "Then the Lord God formed the man of dust from the ground and breathed into his nostrils the breath of life, and the man became a living creature." Jewish law, to this day, says that human life on earth begins with the first breath, as it ends with the last. According to that law, human life means the soul ("nefesh" in Hebrew). For Jews, a fetus becomes animated when it is ensouled. Before that, it is a part of the mother and belongs not to any state but to her and her husband as their property. This chapter will now examine how that information affects laws on abortion in every one of the United States.

The examination will begin with the difference between religion (whether it is monotheistic or not) and agnosticism. Agnostics have not only no belief in a religion but also no need for such a belief. They usually are socialists near the border of Marxist materialistic communism. Materialism is a belief in a world completely and sufficiently devoid of spiritual content. Materialists believe that such content is strictly an illusion without any actual existence. They believe that the core reason people are vulnerable to religious belief is the fear of death. They believe that vendors of religion, preachers in general, take advantage of that vulnerability in peddling their wares. Evangelical preachers on television selling Christianity as the religious savior of your soul beyond death only help strengthen that Marxist materialist belief. Materialists believe that you have no soul to save. The argument for that belief, rather than for its opposite, is the true fanciful argument.

Here is why. Assume that only the material world exists with no need for another, so the three different letters in Albert Einstein's famous equation represent everything that exists:

$$E = MC^2,$$

Where E represents energy, M represents mass, and C represents the speed of light, which involves distance and time.

Explicitly, then, assume that the entire world consists only of those four components: energy, mass, distance, and time. That, however, is obviously not true. If it were true, how would you explain the existence of people and trees or anything else you may see or hear? They have no existence independent of thought, imagery, and ideation. Just where solely in the material universe described by Einstein's equation do your visions, having no measurable dimensions in space or time and no measurable mass or energy, exist? When a person gets an idea, where does it come from? The answer is not the material world. The answer is a spiritual world of shapes, forms, and values that enable people and trees, cars and stars, to exist by creating them out of the material world, just as God created Adam out of dust. That is not a new idea. It goes back in history at least as far as Plato and Moses.

For the whole world even to exist, it needs living creatures who are aware of it, and to be aware of it, those creatures need a soul—a mind—that can create it out of the material world of mass, energy, distance, and time. Psychologically speaking, the soul—the mind—is what transforms sensation into perception. The mind is different from the brain. The interpretation of a person or a tree from the instantaneous and intricate pattern of on-and-off cellular light bulbs in a brain scan is an idea, which, having no mass or other physical measurements, does not exist in the material world. Yet it exists. The indisputability of its existence is indisputable evidence of the separate existence of a world of the mind, a spiritual world separate from but complementary to the material one. The conclusion of this argument is that the spiritual world, by whatever name, must exist, as must religion, which—overlapping with philosophy and psychology—is the study of that world.

This argument is not going to change the minds of Marxist atheists because, in their minds, they have no minds to change. That is how illogically intractable their minds are. That intractability extends over their entire political ideology, which constitutes a belief system tantamount to, horror of horrors, a religion. They worship government rather than God, and today they pray at the shrine of global warming. They recruit young foot soldiers who march obediently and devotedly on their holy path of socialism to their sacred goal of communism, mindless as it is soulless. Logic, which rules in the world of the mind, has no home in their heads. For them, mistreatment of race B by race A is discrimination, but mistreatment of race A by race B is not. Whoever might end up as their leader would have to be the Devil incarnate.

Once again, an irrelevant side note I cannot resist: For years, my wife and I owned a Prius with the license plate MIND. Although we had the only MIND in California, we tried not to let it go to our heads. Sadly, this past year, we lost that Prius with our MIND to a family of rodents who chewed up the vehicle's electrical wires.

Unlike Republicans, Democrats do not believe in evolution because it requires competition, by which you get what you earn. Instead, when in power, their party awards the downtrodden with money robbed by taxation from the people who putatively have been treading over them—not because it is the right thing to do but because, as Willy Horton said about the banks he robbed, that is where the money is. With such a role model, no wonder cities run by Democrats are rife with crime.

Evolution, however, is the way the world works. Charles Darwin discovered that in the animal and plant world. Competitive sports are a metaphor for it. It is what makes artificial intelligence useful by trying out all recorded options and selecting the one that has worked the highest proportion of times. That is what the actual intelligence of a person does though with a more limited availability of options. Despite that imitation, however, a person has a resource that a computer lacks, and that is the world of ideas. An idea can come to a person but not to a computer. The world of ideas is where physicists discover laws that govern the material world. The laws themselves do not exist in the material world, yet that world complies with them. Out of the chaos produced from the Big Bang that physicists and astronomers claim occurred at the time of creation, the tiniest of particles managed over 13.8 billion years of evolution to comply with the laws of physics in the formation of the atoms and molecules, the stars and planets, of the universe today. Who made that happen?

Now, with apologies, I must make another irrelevant side note. For a seventh-grade science class, without knowing the precise meaning or correct pronunciation of the words, I wrote this short poem:

Out of the ab'yss of chaos Like a vast reciprocal ball Came gods Gaea and Uran'us In eternal nothing and all.

By "reciprocal," I meant a tug-of-war between the two

gods.

Just as the world of physics has laws, so does the world of thought. Among them are logic, grammar, and standards of aesthetic and moral value. These laws govern all acts of creativity by thinkers, writers, and artists. Unlike the laws of physics, because people have free will, the laws governing thought are not mandatory. That difference is responsible for much of the misunderstanding and variation of opinion that people have.

So, with the case having been made for religion, how does religion apply to abortion?

Answer: It applies in a big, even determinative, way. That is what the remainder of this chapter is about.

Religion matters so little politically to Democrats that it hardly, if at all, enters their thinking about abortion. Even worse, because religion, at least the Christian religion dominant in our country, restricts or bans abortion, Democrats, with little if any religious qualms, have no trouble endorsing and promoting its unrestricted availability.

If abortion matters to people who value religion,

then an important question to answer is, What do people of different religions think about abortion? Do they all share the Christian view of banning it completely or restricting it to the early weeks of pregnancy? Perhaps, surprisingly, to most Christians, all religions do not share that view. Like Christians, some Muslims share the Catholic view, and some the Protestant view. The Jewish religion shares neither, however. According to Jewish law, as noted earlier, the beginning of human life—ensoulment—occurs at birth, with the first breath. So Jews, at least religiously, require no restriction on abortion at any time during pregnancy.

That exception for Jews is critically important particularly in America. Earlier, this chapter examined the Tenth Amendment to the Constitution to show how it fundamentally supported the Supreme Court decision overturning *Roe v. Wade* and returning the power to regulate abortion to the states. That amendment had a condition apparently ignored by the justices, however. Here is the amendment restated but with a portion of it underlined to identify that condition: *"The powers not delegated to the United States by the Constitution, nor prohibited by it to the states, are reserved to the states respectively, or to the people."*

That condition raises the following critical question: Does the Constitution, in any place, forbid the power of abortion to the states? The answer is, yes, it does in the very first amendment: *"Congress shall make no law respecting an establishment of religion, or prohibiting the free exercise thereof; or abridging the freedom of speech, or of the press; or the right of the people peaceably to* assemble, and to petition the government for a redress of grievances."

Unless any state should allow such a law, which is unthinkable, the free exercise of Jewish law forbids the power to regulate abortion not only to the federal government but also to the states.

This chapter has addressed the relation of abortion to religion. In doing so, it has identified religion with restrictions on abortion and agnosticism or atheism with no restrictions on it. Ironically, instead of dividing believers and nonbelievers on the issue of abortion, religion could bring them together on it, at least here in the United States.

Democrats and Republicans have many issues to battle over, particularly today as the two parties gear up for the 2024 presidential election. Abortion should no longer be one of those issues despite the effect of its loss on both parties. For pro-life Republicans, the loss of all government power to regulate abortion would be a profound disappointment. For Democrats, the loss of abortion as an issue would be an even greater disappointment. Immediately following the Supreme Court decision reversing *Roe v. Wade*, Democrats used the pro-life position of the Republican Party as a powerful weapon against it in the 2022 Congressional election. Abortion was so powerful a weapon that the Democrats won the election in the Senate and very nearly did so in the House despite the blatant failures of the Biden administration that led many people to predict a Republican victory of tsunamic proportions. Now, if abortion should no longer be available as an issue, Democrats would lose that highly effective and critically important weapon.

The issue of abortion in the United States does not belong in politics. It belongs to the Supreme Court. A Jewish person or organization should return it there soon.

CHAPTER 3

The Pandemic

The Pandemic: **Dr. Fauci's Monster**

If I cannot inspire love, I will cause fear!

—Dr. Frankenstein's monster in the book by Mary Shelley

Dr. Frankenstein's man-made monster, the subject of Mary Shelley's novel, demonstrating her considerable skill as a writer, was no more monstrous than Dr. Fauci's, pandemic, though Dr. Fauci has claimed that his monster was born naturally as the grotesque offspring of a human being and a bat—if you can believe it. My own belief is that Dr. Fauci's story of the origin of the pandemic is just one of numerous demonstrations of his considerable skill as a liar. This chapter will open the Pandora's box of those lies and examine some of the ones about the pandemic, including its origin.

Whether it is actually true or not, regardless of your reason for doing it, a lie is something you tell people is true even though you believe it is not true.

Saying something is true that you believe is true even though it is not true is not a lie, nor is it a lie if others believe it is not true regardless of whether it is true or not. Calling something a lie that is not a lie makes you a liar. With that definition in mind, let us now examine who is or who is not a liar on the issues of the pandemic and the 2020 election that occurred in the midst of it. The examination will focus on the contrast of the lying on the two issues.

At the beginning of the pandemic in the United States, in January and February of 2020, a dispute arose over the origin of the virus. In agreement with prominent scientists working in the area, President Trump then believed, as he still believes, that the virus originated in the Wuhan laboratory in China. That laboratory was carrying on so- called gain-of-function research on viruses. The goal of that research is to tweak a virus to increase its transmissibility or virulence among human beings. Success in doing that might lead to success in the opposite direction of making a troubling virus less transmissible or less virulent. At least, that was the justification of the research, which scientists realized could have dangerous consequences if not done with great care. The Wuhan laboratory has had a poor reputation in that regard. The danger of gain-of-function research is so grave that the United States government established a moratorium on funding it in 2014 but, with the urging of government scientists, including Dr. Fauci, rescinded the moratorium in 2017. Following that, the government, with the urging of Dr. Fauci, resumed funding of gain-of-function research at the Wuhan laboratory. The rest of that saga is now history.

Because of the pandemic's rapid spread throughout the world and because of its terrible consequences in illness and death, Dr. Fauci and his fellow government scientists circulated an email encouraging government grant recipients for viral research to promote the belief that the virus originated not in the Wuhan laboratory but in a bat that transmitted it to human beings at a Wuhan wet market near the laboratory. Dr. Fauci, if anyone, likely knows the truth, which an increasing number of people today believe is the Wuhan laboratory rather than the bat. Yet Dr. Fauci still insists that a bat, not Dr. Fauci, was the origin of the pandemic. Whether Dr. Fauci is lying depends on whether he truly believes the bat story, regardless of which of the two stories or even any other is true. Unaware of what Dr. Fauci truly believes, I personally cannot call him a liar though I can understand the motivation to be one. Would you want to admit, even to yourself, that the pandemic would not have occurred without your involvement?

On other issues, the story is much clearer. On the issue of masks, for example, Dr. Fauci has varied his position so many times that it cannot be true every time. At some of those times, he must have been lying about it. At first, according to Dr. Fauci, masks were useless. Then they were necessary. Then they were useful but only under certain conditions. So, my saying that he is a liar on this issue does not make me a liar too.

The difference for the 2020 election could hardly be sharper. When Donald Trump says that the election was stolen from him, most of the media and most of all other Democrats say, without qualification, that he is a liar. The federal government and at least two state governments hold this belief so strongly that they are indicting him on the issue. No one of those people or institutions knows what Trump believes, regardless of whether his belief is true or not. That is why all of them—including most notably the federal government, the Associated Press, and opinion page editors of most newspapers in the country—are, in fact, the true liars when they call Donald Trump a liar. I have no idea of whether those people believe in God or government, but I believe that those of them who profess a belief in God are not only liars but hypocrites as well. When Donald Trump says he believes the 2020 election was stolen, he is not a liar, but others who call him that are themselves the actual liars, whether the election was, in fact, stolen or not.

In his campaign to become the Republican candidate for president, Ron DeSantis has accused Donald Trump of handling the pandemic poorly because he failed to fire Dr. Fauci. Does DeSantis not remember that Trump had put his vice president, Mike Pence, in charge of the pandemic? Maybe DeSantis should redirect his criticism to where it belongs. Does DeSantis also not remember that Trump succeeded in making a vaccine for the virus available in just several months when the normal time for accomplishing that is four or five years? You cannot claim good foresight when your hindsight is so poor.

Dr. Fauci did indeed do a terrible job of informing the public about the virus. DeSantis is correct about that. Dr. Fauci's mishandling of the data on masks was just a start, but it alone had disastrous consequences. Although data worldwide were available early in the pandemic showing that masks were generally unnecessary for healthy people and often ineffective for people who had comorbidities, Dr. Fauci persisted in touting them, even to this day. Masks were particularly unnecessary and even harmful for children at school.

Aside from the hospitalizations and deaths caused during the pandemic directly by the virus, perhaps the most serious damage caused by Dr. Fauci during that time was the closure of schools for up to two years due to his role in keeping the data from the public that healthy children were almost unanimously immune to the virus. That inexplicable and inexcusable mistake will have deleterious consequences for our country and its citizens for generations. National and individual success in the United States depends squarely on a solid educational foundation. As just one of the consequences of the mishandling of the pandemic by Dr. Fauci, that foundation today has become squishier than it has ever been.

Compared with other countries, beginning even before the pandemic, the United States has not been doing well in its education of children with a ranking in the most recently available assessment (2018) by the Programme for International Student Assessment (PISA) of twenty-two out of seventy-four nations in reading, mathematics, and science, only slightly above average, in the combined score. By contrast, China had the highest score. As noted earlier, things have gone downward from there. In a special assessment by the National Center for Education Assessment (NCEA) to assess the effect of school closure during the pandemic, scores for nine-year-old students dropped five points in English and seven points in mathematics, the largest drop in English since 1999 and the first recorded drop in mathematics.

Among the other consequences of the pandemic, the vaccination proclamation cries out for attention. Supported by Dr. Fauci, the administration not only made the vaccination available to the public, continuing that effort begun by the Trump administration, but also, different from the Trump administration, mandated its use. If you did not take it, then the military and other government organizations would discharge you, as would some private organizations as well. Toward the end of the pandemic, about half the adult population had tested positive for the virus and thereby were immune to it but, with the threat of the loss of their jobs, were ordered by the government, whether they were military or civilian, to take the vaccine. Anyone who fails to understand that only a totalitarian government would do that deserves to live under one.

People listening to the news on the three major television networks may be excused from that fate because the news they receive often lacks information that the administration does not want them to have. One glaring omission from the news is the efficacy of natural immunity. That omission, which is unconscionable, has been going on since the beginning of the Biden administration. In two October 2021 letters to my local newspaper, *The Monterey County Herald*, I addressed that problem. Here is the first of those letters, printed there on the twenty-sixth:

What ever happened to natural immunity? About half the adult US population has it because of having contracted one of the variants of the COVID-19 virus. Yet a federal mandate requires that all adults receive at least one vaccination or else. That "or else" can be more consequential than even contracting the virus, especially if you are in good health. If you are an adult, you can lose your job. If you are a child, you can be expelled from school. Those are not all the problems the mandate can produce.

If you have natural immunity and receive the vaccination, you are vulnerable to heart complications because of your oversupply of antibodies. Most children have natural immunity. So parents must think at least twice before permitting vaccinations for their children. This information comes from Johns Hopkins University. It obviously conflicts with the information from the federal government, which, for whatever reason, ignores natural immunity.

Every immune person, adult or child, who receives a vaccination takes that vaccination away from someone outside the US whose government has only a limited supply of vaccinations, if any. Only by increasing that supply can anyone in the world be free of the development of a new strain for which even our current vaccinations won't work. Mandated vaccinations make no sense; they are unwise and dangerous.

Federal vaccination mandates are also unconstitutional. So why do we have them?

Here is the second, which *The Herald* refused to print:

Letters in the October 30 *Herald* question Johns Hopkins University as a source of information I cited in my October 26 letter about vaccination versus natural immunity protection against the delta variant of COVID-19. Here are additional sources that confirm that information:

According to the October 14 *Austin American-Statesman*, "Georgia Tech researchers, using COVID-19 case estimates from the US Centers for Disease Control and Prevention, estimate that as of October 9, 52 percent of the US population had been infected."

According to the prestigious journal *Science*, "The natural immune protection that develops after a SARS-CoV-2 infection offers considerably more of a shield against the delta variant of the pandemic coronavirus than two doses of the Pfizer-BioNTech vaccine, according to a large Israeli study." According to CDC researchers, "Since April 2021, there have been increased reports...of cases of inflammation of the heart...happening after mRNA COVID-19 vaccination

(Moderna and Pfizer) in the United States...particularly in adolescents and young adults."

That addendum "particularly in adolescents and young adults"—who are likelier to have natural immunity than older adults—suggests that vaccination of children who are even more likely to have natural immunity to COVID-19 could lead to heart complications in them, as I cautioned in my letter.

My position in that letter was not against vaccinations per se; it was against punitive government mandates of them for adults or children.

Dr. Martin Makary of Johns Hopkins University has been a voice in the wilderness on this issue, wilderness to too many people being the Fox News Network.

When the government or the news media omit consequential information intentionally, they are not providing the public with the truth. Unless you tell the whole truth, without consequential omission, you are lying. That is precisely and unfortunately what the federal government and the three major television news networks have been doing on the issue of the pandemic, if not on other politically controversial issues as well.

The federal government has not only kept consequential information about the virus from the public; it has also dangerously misled the public with misinformation about the virus. The federal government promoted testing for the virus and provided statistics about the number of people in every community of the country who tested positive, as if that were universally a terrible thing when, in fact, it was a good thing if you did not suffer any serious symptoms or require hospitalization.

Because hospitals tested every entering patient for the virus regardless of the reason for entry, they could have exaggerated the number hospitalizations and deaths due to the virus by counting patients who tested positive but entered for other health reasons, including injuries resulting from accidents, as COVID-19 casualties.

In fact, though the federal government kept it a secret, your testing positive for the virus made you immune to it, even more so than your taking the vaccine, as noted earlier. Even today, as of this writing in September 2023, the federal government has just approved a new version of the vaccine and is actively promoting it for everyone over six months of age. The public has fortunately been getting wise to the federal government—especially in view of the vaccine' possible side effects—and is mostly ignoring the   administration's television advertisements encouraging its use.

Can we put a label on such behavior by the federal government or any of its agencies? Yes, we can. We can label it for what it is: "deception for gain" (in money, votes, or anything else of value to the person or organization that commits it) or, in a single word, "fraud." Legally, that deception can consist of intentionally providing or relying upon inaccurate or incomplete information while knowingly being uncertain of its accuracy or completeness. Without scrutiny by the media, the number of federal government actions that qualify under this definition must be enormous.

As important as the question might be of why a government commits fraud, an even more urgent question is, What can we citizens do to stop it? Governments are responsible for protecting their citizens from fraud. When they fail to do that and, worse, when they themselves commit fraud, then they are subject to legal action brought by the people against whom the fraud is committed. In this case, that would include the entire population of the country. Because no organization other than the federal government itself represents the entire population, what appears necessary to bring the case to court, if the president or Congress will not do it, is a class-action lawsuit brought by an organization that represents at least one subgroup of the population affected by fraudulent behavior perpetrated by a particular government agency, which would be the target of the legal action.

Here are a number of possibilities for that action: a veterans' organization like the American Legion could sue the Defense Department for its fraudulent discharge of military members who refused to take the vaccine, a parents' organization like Moms for Liberty could sue the Centers for Disease Control for its fraudulent school-closure mandate during the pandemic, the Catholic Church could sue the Federal Bureau of Investigation for fraudulently treating pro-life demonstrators as domestic terrorists, or the Republican National Committee could sue state legislatures that fraudulently permitted the Democratic Party, with the pandemic as an excuse, to use voting procedures in the 2020 presidential election that, contrary to "Article II: Section 1," of the Constitution, the legislatures had not authorized.

Such legal cases are not common. Usually, when an administration does something that Congress had not authorized, the two use the Supreme Court to settle their differences. In these cases, Congress represents all the people. When Congress fails to act, however, what recourse do citizens have other than to go to court themselves, represented by groups having legal standing and financial resources to do so? Now is such a time. With representation of both parties so nearly equal in both houses, Congress has been paralyzed from redressing grievances by members of either party. Now is the time to act despite limited precedence for guidance.

All the lawsuits do not have to succeed. Merely their existence, particularly in large numbers, can have the sought-after results. Look at how much Donald Trump rose in the Republican nomination polls each time he faced an indictment, and at the time of this writing, no trial has even yet begun. Large numbers get media attention, and large numbers, informed by that attention, get the attention of government, especially as we get closer to the 2024 presidential election.

To say the pandemic has had a dreadful effect on our country's economy would seem to be a true statement, but it is not. What is a true statement is that the government's handling of the pandemic has had that effect. The mandates by federal and state governments to control the pandemic are responsible for our economic problems.

As a mirror image of the rise and fall of COVID-19 test results, employment numbers have fallen and risen during the course of the pandemic. When they were low, the Biden administration began handing out free money to enable people to live without working. That is never a good thing for a government to do. People have got used to living without working or living without having to go to work while working at home. Money in the hands of people who do not provide goods and services makes their costs rise because of their consequent scarcity. That is inflation whose rightward rise in a bell- shaped curve since the beginning of the current administration has yet to level off, let alone begin to decline. The costs of food and energy, which are not taken into account in that curve, just keep on rising. People are maxing out their credit cards just to live. The Federal Reserve's raising of interest rates to reverse the current adverse trends only adds to the cost while reducing the standard of living. Prediction of the future of our economy is, at best, uncertain.

Just as government leaders have become used to autocratic rule in their mandates to control the pandemic, so, during the same period, college graduates have become used to living without paying their student loans and workers, particularly teachers, have become used to getting paid without going to work. These habits are going to be hard to break. Attributed to St. Paul and later cited by Vladimir Lenin, hardly soulmates, the following aphorism appearing in the New Testament must be true: "He who does not work, neither shall he eat." In fact, that is a fundamental tenet of economics. Adam's sons had to work as farmers and shepherds if they were to have food to eat. That was then, you might argue, but today, we have money to buy such things. That is true, but money loses its value when nothing is available to buy because nobody is working to provide it. Like its educational shadow, the economic shadow of the pandemic may be a long one.

When atheist Vladimer Lenin agrees with a saint, why do Democrats leaning leftward toward Lenin not follow his advice? Why does their government keep on supporting people who do not work? Is the vote of those people worth taking down the whole economy and, with it, the entire country? The feeling of power that political leaders may have acquired from the pandemic will disappear like their echo when they shout out orders on a high hill to an empty valley below. Democrats must grow up or wake up to avoid that comic-tragic outcome. If that does not happen, which appears increasingly likely, then Republicans must do everything possible to win the 2024 presidential election. Today, all we have is hope that Democrats may have not brought the house down before then.

Scarcity is not the only thing that keeps prices high. Neither is the sloth just discussed. Greed always has its foot in the door. Large pharmaceutical companies, so-called Big Pharma, defend the high prices they charge for drugs in this country, in contrast to the much lower prices they charge in other countries, by claiming they need the money to maintain the research productivity that has, over more than a century, vastly improved the health of the entire world. That argument sounds good, but it is not true. Much, if not most, of that productivity occurs not in their laboratories but in the laboratories of universities both here and abroad. Other than education, universities do not sell anything. So where do their laboratories get the money to support the research they do? The answer is mostly grants from the federal government, particularly from the Centers for Disease Control, where Dr. Fauci had reigned until recently for some forty years. That is where the Wuhan laboratory got money to do the gain-of-function research that likely produced the pandemic.

That being the case, then what does Big Pharma do with the money it gets from the overcharged portions of their drug prices? That money, of course, goes to shareholders, bonuses for high corporate executives, advertisements (i.e., all those ads on television) and, of course, to lobbying. The Centers for Disease Control sits at the top of an inverted V, with one leg in Big Pharma and one leg in academia. Big Pharma money flows up its leg to lobby government scientists like Dr. Fauci at the top, and United States taxpayer money goes down the other leg to support professors, their graduate students, and their research assistants at universities. So Big Pharma greed makes taxpayers pay twice to support the drug-research industry: once when they buy the drug and once again when they pay their federal income taxes. That is quite a double whammy.

Politically, the pandemic could have no greater consequence than it had on the 2020 presidential election. Until the pandemic hit the world in January of 2020, the Trump administration had been such a success that hardly any doubt could exist that Trump would win that election. He did not, and the pandemic was the major reason why.

Of course, Democrats were doing everything possible to assure that result, but without the pandemic, they had little, if any, chance of success. To say the pandemic could be your friend sounds ridiculous, but it was anything but ridiculous for Democrats. In fact, in 2020, it was their best friend.

Because of the election result, it was also the best friend of China, where it began. Trump was a huge roadblock to China's achievement of its economic and political plans. With Trump gone and a business partner like Biden in the White House, the lights in China were burning bright again. Could China have foreseen that result, it would, no doubt, have deliberately created the pandemic though, more likely, its beginning there was an accident. The same could not be so readily said for the Democrats, the advent of the pandemic being so good for them. Democrats and their news media accomplices have lionized Dr. Fauci as if they knew that without him, the pandemic might never have occurred. Dr. Fauci is a Democrat. So to say Democrats are responsible for the pandemic would be incorrect only to the extent of the difference between the singular and the plural of their name.

To end where we began this chapter, Dr. Frankenstein's monster had a soul; Dr. Fauci's does not.

Responsible for almost seven million deaths worldwide, with over a million of them in the United States, even if for nothing else, the pandemic is indeed a monster, and no punishment is long enough and harsh enough for Dr. Fauci to suffer for his role in the creation and care of this monster.

CHAPTER 4

Sex and Gender

Sex and Gender: **Two Different Worlds**

Responding to a boy who, in 1958, wrote to an advice column in Ebony Magazine, "I feel about boys the way I ought to feel about girls," Dr. Martin Luther King responded as follows: "Your feeling toward boys is probably not an innate tendency, but...culturally acquired. Your reasons for adopting the habit have now been consciously suppressed or unconsciously repressed. Therefore, it is necessary to deal with this problem by getting back to some of the experiences and circumstances that led to the habit...I would suggest that you see a good psychiatrist who can assist you in this effort."

Whatever happened to debauchery, depravity, lasciviousness, and perversion? They have all vanished into thin air, like natural immunity, simply by fiat. Seemingly by the snap of a finger, they are all gone. Not the behavior, though, just the words. Like all the other putative accomplishments by the Biden administration, the words are all that count. "Change the words, and you change the world" is its mantra. For the materialists that Democrats as a party have become, appearances astonishingly supersede facts. Sex between a man and a woman is not the whole story for them, and the story is what counts even though in the real world, sex between a man and a woman is the only form of sex, its natural form, that is necessary for humanity to survive. All other forms of sex not only contribute nothing to the survival of the species but also to the extent that they replace the natural form, even threaten its survival.

Democrats keep on adding to their list of unnatural forms of sex. LGBT has now been joined by Q as one for good measure. Democrats, of course, did not invent those forms, and they do not include the only people who practice them, but they have removed the shame from them and have the distinction of including the only people in the nation who not only extol them as an art form but also, like wine tasters, have become connoisseurs of them. They extol behavior today not only for which people once were stoned, drawn, and quartered or made to wear scarlet letters to identify and humiliate them in public but also for which whole villages of them like Sodom and Gomorrah were burned to the ground.

Instead of condemning LGBTQ, Democrats celebrate it with rainbow flags flown in blue-state schools and Gay Pride Month observed nationally. Even some businesses have joined the celebration—Disney World, Anheuser-Busch (Budweiser), and Target being notable among them—though, in doing so, they have dropped their bottom line and almost lost their pants. Normal people apparently just do not get it.

Turning bad into good and good into bad seems to be what Democrats believe to be their destiny. Turning the world of words upside down seems to be their revolution.

How strange it is for a materialistic party that denies the existence of a spiritual world to distinguish between sex and gender! Sex exists in the physical world whether in the form of a noun as a physical characteristic or in the form of a verb as a physical act, but where is gender in this world? Can it be seen or heard? What are its physical dimensions and its mass? It has none. It exists only as an ethereal idea in another world, whatever its name might be. Mind? Or, heaven forbid for materialistic Democrats, heaven? Wherever it exists, it certainly does not exist on earth. Yet Democrats use gender all the time to parse out and celebrate all the components of LGBTQ. Traditionally, as well as naturally, gender has been a two-valued scale for sex, the two values being male and female. Now Democrats have redefined the scale as continuous, like a rainbow, extending from extreme male (hostile masculinity?) on the left to extreme female (loving femininity?) on the right, with most people somewhere in between. Supposedly, the people in between are the ones who can get into the queer relationships of LGBTQ—the people who today indicate "other" on personal-information forms allowing continuous gender as a choice. A gay woman (L) would score on the male side, and a gay man (G) would score on the female side of the gender scale while a binary person (B) would score in the middle. The *L*s and the *G*s have been a part of humanity ever since we obtained free will. The *T*s are what are new and are also what are most controversial today.

Prior to modern medicine, a person had to remain the same sex physically throughout life. Now physicians can transform (the *T* in LGBTQ being for trans) people physically from one side of the gender scale to the other though not to the same extent back again. The controversy focuses on two issues: whether parents or schools can authorize the transformation of children who choose to have one and whether transgendered men can participate in female sports. With the resolution of the second issue being obvious to anyone who has common sense, the focus here will be on the first issue.

Traditionally and (to most people) obviously, parents rather than schools should make decisions having lifelong consequences for their children. So what a surprise parents must have had during the pandemic when they learned from homeschooling their children that schools were making transgender decisions for them with neither the consent nor the knowledge of their parents! That was not all parents learned in their homeschooling experience. They also learned that, with library books for backup, curricula for the early elementary- school years included instruction not only on natural sex but also on its unnatural forms, as though all were acceptable alternatives, and their instruction was age-appropriate.

In response to that discovery, parents have begun to protest at meetings of school boards and even to run for membership on them in attempts to guide the schools back to normalcy. Likely, the most effective response of parents will prove to be their organization into groups, like Moms for Liberty, to oppose not only the schools but also the federal government whose Department of Justice has had the Federal Bureau of Investigation haunt and hunt them down as "domestic terrorists."

Teachers are experts in academic curricula. They are knowledgeable about the age-appropriateness of traditional academic curricula, like the three *R*s. They are not experts in emotional development. Teachers may still give grades on achievement on one side and on comportment on the other side of report cards, as they did when I was in school. Assessment of comportment, however, is not the same as assessment of emotional development. Though not the province of teachers, emotional development is important. Simply to say that, however, would be a gross understatement. Emotional development, traditionally and appropriately the province of parents, is critical to life itself. In justification of that statement, I am going to provide information about childhood emotional development without citing its sources. To avoid distraction, the source citation will come later.

Different from other animals, human beings lack instincts that would have enabled them to survive independently as young adults at about three to five years old. If we had instincts guiding our behavior, we would not have to go to school. Not having instincts, we must slow down our growth for several years, called a latency stage, during which we learn skills that enable us to survive independently as adults. That is a stage, from about five to twelve years old, when we learn not only to read and write and learn mathematics from addition to long division but also when we learn to be boys and girls. Interference in that learning at any time during the latency stage—whether by adults or other children—can be disastrous for life afterward.

Near the beginning and end of the latency stage are times, called critical periods, when children are particularly sensitive to such interference, particularly involving emotional development, including gender orientation. Many people believe people are born with their gender orientation as male or female. That is not true. One quarter of identical twins do not share the same gender orientation if one of them is gay or lesbian. Something must have differed in their environment to cause their differing gender orientations, and that something most likely occurred during the early or late critical periods. That is why, to assure normal emotional development, schools must have a strictly hands-off policy on gender instruction during the elementary-school years.

Those years are a time when children naturally take a vacation from sexual interests to develop normally as boys and girls. In fact, they typically avoid one another and play solely in single-sex groups. Of course, that all ends when they reach adolescence, often with a positive bang but not always. For some children, the latency stage ends with emotional distress likely caused by an unwelcome emotional experience that occurred just before or just after the beginning of their latency stage and that they could no longer repress, at least completely. For gay children, that experience was likely sexual, the result being imprinted rather than inherited. Schools and the government agencies that administer them have no business in creating an environment that increases the likelihood of such an experience.

When a government agency seeks to create such an environment, a fair question to ask is, Why? Ignorance cannot be the answer. The effort is too great for that. The government must have a solid reason for doing something so dangerous. The most obvious reason is to get votes from a voter minority, even if it is no larger than 7 or 8 percent, recent elections being so close.

The voter minority also has an interest in promoting itself, and it can do that by influencing school curricula in its favor. Homosexuality begins at a young age. The queer community must know that. It likely believes that by putting a positive spin on being gay, schools can encourage children who are undecided to move in its direction. Its flying rainbow flags and celebrating Gay Pride Month certainly encourage that movement. Moms for Liberty and its sister movements cannot act too quickly to stop it. Nor can the voters. If for no other reason, we should move the Democrats out of the White House and Congress and as far away from Washington, DC, as possible. The 2024 election cannot come soon enough.

A psychologist might describe the latency stage as a time during child development not only when the most active drives are curiosity and strengthening natural sexual orientation but also when the sexual drive is repressed and even denied though it too is, while unconscious, growing increasingly strong.

Homosexuality is not the only personality disorder that can develop during the latency stage. Others, even more troubling, are obsessive-compulsive disorder and schizophrenia. What may happen to children in such cases is that an event occurs sometime during the latency stage, usually in the second half, that threatens to release the sexual drive before they have developed sufficiently to cope with it. The event is especially threatening if it revives the feelings of dread and helplessness the children had had during a traumatic experience in a critical period shortly before or after the onset of the latency stage, an event so traumatic that they had repressed it. In any event, the children feel helpless to control unknown and unwelcome impulses and usually have fearful nightmares that they do not understand and cannot prevent.

To cope, the children may thrash about with superstitious and compulsive behavior like counting routines, in which they repeat a common activity a specific number of times, or avoid walking on lines separating segments of a sidewalk, a superstition so common it has a name: "Walk on a crack, break your grandmother's back." The children may avoid a certain person, adult or child, in the belief that person may be the one who is controlling them somehow, possibly by hypnotism. Usually, though the trauma and irrational behavior subside as the children grow old enough to cope with the problem, its scars may remain as irrational personality traits like excessive cleanliness or exaggerated fear of germs, a fear many people were familiar with during the pandemic.

Less commonly but unfortunately, the irrational behavior prior to the end of the latency stage may grow into an obsessive-compulsive disorder or the belief in control by others may reemerge in early adulthood as paranoia and other manifestations of schizophrenia. One or more sexually abnormal traumatic experiences occurring in the critical period near the beginning of the latency stage could, without professional counseling, develop during that stage into homosexuality. Teachers who intervene in the emotional development of children during the latency stage are not just playing with fire; they are committing psychological arson.

All the preceding psychological observations have their origin in the works of Sigmund Freud (psychoanalysis), Konrad Lorenz (imprinting), and Benjamin Spock in his book *Baby and Child Care*. Now in its tenth edition, that book should be a must-read for anyone rearing or teaching a child. When I took a course in child psychology as a college sophomore in 1949, the first edition of that book was one of the course's two textbooks. The current edition is much more reader-friendly than the first and much less explicitly Freudian by avoidance of technical terms, its being written in a common-sense and easily understandable style.

Freud is well-known for his indication of the importance of the latency stage to sexual development. Lorenz is famous for his demonstration of imprinting and its critical period in goslings who, not being brought up by their mother, learned to follow him around by imprinting on him instead of her during a limited, critical period sometime after hatching. Since then—the mid-nineteen thirties—and even prior to then, studies have shown that imprinting can occur in other animals, including human beings.

My information about the latency stage comes not only from reading and lectures but also from personal experience. I spent my entire latency stage in a Los Angeles Jewish neighborhood during the Great Depression. As I recall my experience then, I was, for my sex, a typical, even professional, child of that place and time.

Except when it rained, my mother sent me out to play immediately after I brought my lunch pail home from school. Still, I found time and places to read comic books voraciously. I practiced with yo-yos during the yo-yo season. I played marbles at the local playground. I listened to a librarian who, outside under a weeping willow tree on the other side of a fence from the playground, read stories aloud to children sitting on the lawn in front of her on Saturday mornings.

I was a member of four different gangs, sometimes two of them simultaneously, which occasionally fought mock battles with each other in places like open foundations of houses not completely built because of the Depression or after a rain on hills where we could pull clods of wet grass from the ground and hurl them at one another. I made weapons like match shooters out of clothespins and rubber guns out of used tire inserts. I made scooters out of apple crates and roller skates. I roller-skated just for fun or when I had to travel far to a swimming hole near Alhambra or to downtown Los Angeles where I bought old pennies for my coin collection. I covered my whole body with ashes from incinerators in an attempt to become invisible, which worked no better than my attempt to fly by pulling a rope over the handle of a large handmade wooden basket while I sat in it.

I sold magazines and newspapers and shined shoes and mowed lawns to earn money—pennies for the magazines and newspapers and nickels for the shoes and lawns. When I went door-to-door doing those things on some evenings during warm months, I did not miss a single word of Jack Benny's or Fred Allen's radio programs because I could hear them as I walked house to house, all with their windows open to keep cool. Almost every day, when I rounded up my brothers and brought them home for dinner, the two older of us needed baths. I was indeed living the life of a typical, even professional, male child until just before I turned ten years old.

Suddenly then, without warning, I began to have a repeated nightmare of a black metal structure slowly falling straight down toward me while I could do nothing to stop it. I did not tell my parents about it. Instead, I tried to cope with it myself. Having no rational way of doing that, I resorted to superstitious behavior like repeating an activity a specific number of times or avoiding sidewalk lines, just as described in the book by Dr. Spock that I read later in college. As Dr. Freud might have predicted, I avoided a specific boy and a specific girl because I thought they would hypnotize me to do something I did not want to do. Now, instead of being a typical male child, I became a typical psychological wreck.

How could I explain that? At the time, of course, I could not, but after I began that college course in child psychology, it all began to make sense.

When I was five years old, during a critical period just before I entered the latency stage, I had my tonsils removed. That was one of the most traumatic experiences of my life. To put me asleep, the doctor pressed a large metal plunger over my face to force me to breathe gas. I yelled and screamed and vainly fought his attempt to do that. Unknown to me at the time, instead of its normal disappearance, I was experiencing an event that marked the end of whatever romantic feelings I might have had for my mother as punishment for my having had them, consciously or unconsciously, in the first place.

Later, that trauma returned in the form of recurring nightmares, which began shortly after I had a tooth extraction because the dentist doing the extraction used the same method of putting me to sleep that the doctor had used for my tonsillectomy. This time, though I was too old to yell and scream, I felt the same dread and helplessness I had felt the first time.

Fortunately, for me, the second traumatic experience occurred late enough in my latency period that its effect on me did not intensify or last long though, to me, at the time, it seemed unbearable and forever. By the time I was eleven and no longer resisting entry into adolescence, it was all gone except for a scar of obsessive concern with hygiene, which I shared with my father and which helped me to identify with him.

That psychological scar slowly grew smaller on its own as I grew older until now when it is so nearly normal that I even become irritated with other people's compulsive behavior of wearing masks and testing for COVID-19 months after the pandemic.

Human beings, being social animals, psychological symptoms and diagnoses, like the clothes we wear, come in and go out of fashion. Though once relatively common among psychiatric disorders, for example, hysteria and catatonia hardly ever occur now. Cyclic disorder, particularly its depression pole, is the one in vogue today. Rather than the latency stage, adolescence is the time when that condition brews. That is the time when sex and competition, along with independence, are the most active drives. Lack of self-esteem is then the psychological problem, to which, because of competition, at least half of all adolescents are vulnerable. When extreme, lack of self-esteem can express itself psychotically as either depression or delusions of grandeur, the other pole of cyclic disorder, sometimes also called bipolar disorder.

Depression is the normal direction, but when it becomes extreme, the irrational reaction can be either suicide or, in the other direction, the development of delusions of grandeur. Some people become so sensitized to depression that even when it shows its early signs, they go in that other direction, toward the manic pole, so that—like depression, though less often—their condition appears unipolar rather than bipolar. Tragically increasing in frequency now together with suicide is mass murder of perceived competitors when the repressed self-hatred underlying lack of self-esteem is released and, being unbearable to oneself, is redirected, wholly or partially, to them.

This discussion may appear to be off message in a chapter on sex and gender, but it is not. The T for transgender in LBGTQ is developmentally and consequentially different from the L and G there. The L and G are disorders of the mind that, once established, are difficult, if not impossible to change, particularly after the latency stage. Like cyclic disorder, the transgender problem occurs both as a fad and in the mind, not the body. Yet psychiatrists treat the two conditions materially, in the case of cyclic disorder typically with lithium, commonly taken as a pill, when both conditions—my point here—should receive mental rather than physical treatment.

For the transgender problem, which psychiatrists call gender- identity disorder or gender dysphoria, the treatment *de jour* consists of the physical and dangerously unnatural sexual alteration of a body. Sex and gender exist in two different worlds. Physical treatment of a mental illness—and that is what gender-identity disorder is—cannot cure the problem simply because the problem is not physical. All physical treatment does is affect the physical expression of the problem in the brain—which is not the same as the mind—and in behavior. Like for a problem of low self-esteem, the appropriate treatment for a sexual-identity problem is psychological counseling, not surgery or pills. The problem exists in the mental world, not the physical or material one.

Teachers aware of a transgender problem in a child should inform the child's parents, not a school administrator, about it. The problem is a family problem, not a school problem. School problems, like too- large or too-readiness-diverse classes, arise in the provision of intellectual skills that enable children to participate usefully and successfully as grown-ups in the world of work. In the early school years, those skills are reading, writing, and arithmetic, including, today, doing those things on a computer.

Discussion of the issue of gender identity in public was unnecessary prior to the 2020 presidential election. What is it about the current administration that makes the discussion necessary now? That is a question that demands an answer as soon as possible, prior to the next election, because gender identity has become one of the salient issues currently troubling voters. Like racial injustice, Democrats have made it a political issue simply to obtain votes from minority groups. That is hypocritical, irresponsible, and dangerous.

Democracy to Democrats has come to mean equity of outcome for everyone regardless of skill or effort or normality of behavior. Equity has become their self-identified cause. Since winners breed losers, for Democrats, competition must go. Republicans, who promote competition, are therefore bad, and so they also must go. Democrats seek not to be merely a majority party; they seek to be the *only* party. The party that has that goal is the one that truly must go because the achievement of that goal is the achievement of the destruction of democracy and its replacement by single-party, totalitarian rule. Democrats' identification of themselves as members of the party opposing the destruction of democracy by the other party is not just ironic; it is deplorable. Like almost, if not all, of everything else Democrats proclaim they represent or do, the very opposite has turned out to be true since they gained political power in 2020. Not only must Democrats fail to win power again in 2024 but they also must either do a 180-degree turnaround or, that unfortunately being unlikely, rename themselves for what they have tragically become, the Communist Party of America.

CHAPTER 5

Global Warming

Global Warming: **Lying with Statistics**

Reworked for a general readership, this chapter presents what I wrote for the American Journal of Theoretical and Applied Statistics *in its third issue of volume 11 published in 2022.*

A November 2021 article I wrote for the *American Statistical Association* journal *Chance* on a misuse of statistics by hydrogeologists in their modeling of water levels belowground raised the question in my mind of whether climatologists might be committing the same statistical errors in their modeling of global warming aboveground. The research reported in this chapter provides and discusses the answer to that question.

Both communities of scientists, hydrogeologists and climatologists, use the same kind of model. At a specific time and zone of a stacked checkerboard of zones, which, in climatology, covers the whole earth upward in the atmosphere and downward in the oceans, the models involved break down an observed measurement—of water level in hydrogeology and temperature in climatology—into predicted and error components. In that breakdown, the predicted component is a weighted sum of observed or estimated values indicating, for each value, the positive or negative extent to which it might affect the observed measurement -- good examples being well-pumping rate in hydrogeology and number of parts per million of airborne carbon dioxide (CO_2) molecules in climatology. Like the observed measurements, the values for the influences can vary over time and from zone to zone while the weights remain constant over all times and zones. In model development, based on the observed measurements and values representing the influences for all times and zones, the weights are determined to minimize the random error variation while keeping the average error and the correlation between predicted and error components equal to zero.

That all seems reasonable, so what could go wrong in either case? What went wrong in each is that to reduce the random error variation further or to achieve a desired result, scientists altered some of the influence values within a generally agreed-upon range, the alteration possibly differing from scientist to scientist. Somewhat a source of confusion, the two research communities use different names for the alteration process: "calibration" in hydrogeology and "tuning" in climatology. The trouble with doing that, by whatever name, is that it creates an impermissible negative correlation between predicted and error components, errors being unpredictable, by having to subtract from the predicted component what it adds to the error component or add to the predicted component what it subtracts from the error component to avoid altering the observed measurement, which is their sum.

The effect of that negative correlation between predicted and error components is to exaggerate predictions so they tend to be too high when predictions rise because errors fall (tending to be negative) then and too low when predictions fall because errors rise (tending to be positive) then.

As figure 1 shows, that is, in fact, what happened in a specific project involving the modeling of water levels by hydrogeologists. The question now is whether the same thing has occurred in the modeling of temperatures by climatologists.

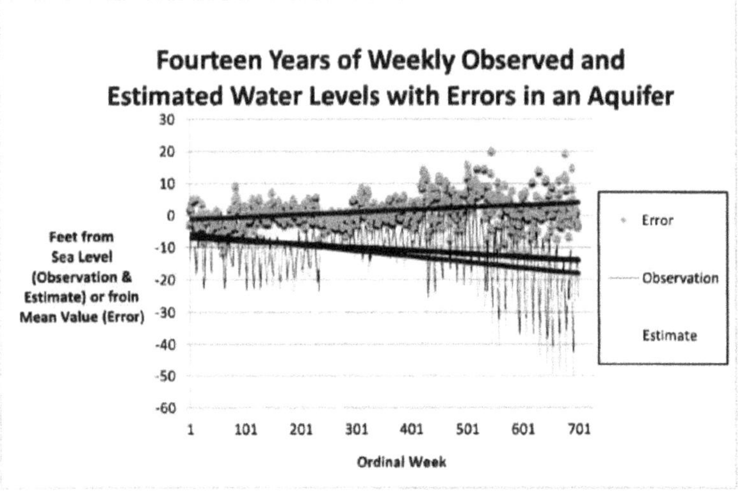

Figure 1. Calibrated model predictions (gray, jagged line) of observed water levels (black, jagged line) with errors (filled, gray circles) over time. The heavy straight lines show (top to bottom) the corresponding error, observation, and prediction trends.

Exploration of the answer to that question can benefit from a corresponding exploration of figure 1, which shows that errors go up (from negative to positive) as water levels go down over time. Because errors, by definition, should not be predictable, the nonzero correlation between errors and water levels was so troubling that the project abandoned the use of the model to predict water levels. The hydrogeologist making that decision based it on the belief that the observed change in water level over time was too fast for the model to catch up. If that were true, the model would be overpredicting water levels when, as shown in figure 1, it is underpredicting them: The bottom trend line (for predictions) is lower than the middle trend line (for observations). So what is the real problem?

Though based on virtually the same data, figure 1 is not the figure shown in the official report on the project. The figure in that report shows the errors trending downward rather than upward. That is because the hydrogeologist who created the figure in the report determined errors by subtracting observations from predictions rather than vice versa, which is the correct way to do it and which is the way the errors shown in figure 1 were determined. That mistake was not trivial. It prevented the hydrogeologist from discerning the actual cause of the nonzero correlation between errors and declining water levels over time.

The cause for the rise of errors with the decline of water levels is that when water levels go down, predictions follow them down, as shown by the bottom two trend lines in figure 1. Meanwhile, as shown by the top trend line there, errors—being negatively correlated with predictions because of calibration—go up. The cause of the worrisome nonzero correlation is not the model; the cause is the calibration of the model. The hydrogeologist, not the model, is the real problem.

Can the same be said about at least some climatologists in their modeling of world temperature over time? Where I found the answer is in the recent book *Unsettled: What Climate Science Tells Us, What It Doesn't, and Why It Matters* by physicist Steven E. Koonin, with particular attention to chapter 4 on modeling. I found the answer there to be yes. Figure 2, which is a copy of figure 4.5 in Koonin's book, shows rising observed and predicted mean-global-surface- temperature "anomalies" over time for twenty-six different models, where the anomalies are departures from the mean global surface temperature between 1880 and 1910. (Koonin, in *Unsettled*, cites the original 2020 source of figure 2, which is the source of the copy shown here.) Each plotted point is an eleven-year average. The four dark-black lines represent separate sets of observations, and the twenty-six light-black lines represent the twenty-six model predictions, which tend to follow the observations. Among other things, the models generally vary in their tuning practices.

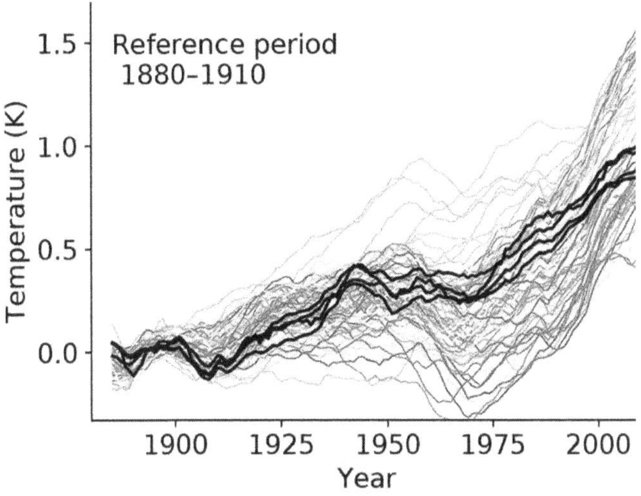

Figure 2. Tuned model predictions (26 gray lines) of observed temperatures (4 black lines) with the apparent gray swath showing the trend of the bulk of the predictions over time.

The apparent gray swath weaving around the four black lines and encompassing the bulk of the model predictions represents them as a group, whereas the substantial variation of the model predictions provides some credence for Koonin's choice of the title for his book, *Unsettled*.

From about 1970, both the observations and the predictions in figure 2 show a rather steep rise in mean global surface temperature, now popularly identified as "global warming." As the use of tuning might predict, the rise is steeper for the predictions than for the observations: Just as calibration resulted in underestimation of falling water levels, so here tuning results in overestimation of rising temperatures. How much is that overestimation? Koonin, toward the end of chapter 4 in *Unsettled*, provides information that may suggest an answer to that question. In a so-called budget analysis, he compared the mean global temperature rise over the past 140 years with total human and natural "forcings" (influence values measured in watts per square meter) that occurred during the same period and, after some correction of the data, showed that model tuning may have led to overestimating the effect of human influences on global warming by a factor no lower than two.

Like the word "forcings" printed within quotation marks in the preceding paragraph, terminology varies among statisticians and users of statistics in different fields. That variation can obscure the occurrence of mistakes in the use of statistics by nonstatisticians.

Terms used for the weights in predictions consisting of weighted sums provide an apt example. Some simply refer to the weights as constants. Statisticians call them parameters, and that could lead a statistician to misinterpret the term "parameter adjustment" when used by hydrogeologists and climatologists. The statistician might think that term meant the development of a new model, with new weights, to reduce error variation. The reason for that misinterpretation is that hydrogeologists and climatologists understand the word "parameter" to mean not a weight but the value representing the influence to which the weight applies. By "parameter adjustment," they mean adjustment of influence values, not constants—in other words, the adjustment of data. So what terms do hydrogeologists and climatologists use to identify a model's weights? Interestingly, they both use the same term: "sensitivities."

The sensitivity that is of particular interest in the study of global warming is the weight that applies to the concentration of CO_2 in the atmosphere. The modelers producing the predictions shown in figure 2 generally agree that the "equilibrium" value (Equilibrium Model

Sensitivity or EMS) of that sensitivity should be equal to about 3.0 degrees centigrade (C). That means that doubling the concentration of CO_2 in the atmosphere from its value prior to the use of fossil fuels would increase the mean global temperature by about 3.0°C, provided no other influences—which, as noted earlier, climatologists call "forcings"—were affecting it. In agreement with Koonin's budget analysis, the different slopes of the curves for the predicted and observed surface temperatures in figure 2 show that 3.0°C might be too high, likely by a factor equal at least to two.

In support of that likelihood, the actual sensitivity for CO_2 concentration in climatology models (called Transient Climate Response or TCR) over the years, prior to subsidence of theorized transient cooling effects, has tended to hover from model to model around 1.5°C, half the 3.0°C EMS, according to Koonin, who cites others in support of that or even a lower number. Climatologists generally believe that the EMS of 3.0°C is the correct long-term value for the CO_2 sensitivity because transient conditions, though unmeasured, might tend to lower the steepness of observation curves. Typical among those conditions are changing cloud formations, decreasing aerosol emissions, and melting icebergs. Perhaps even more than to improve the fit of their models to data, climatologists use tuning to help guide their development of models having TSR values that are increasingly close to their EMS. That, in fact, may be a common practice.

Although almost all the models cited in the 113 pages of a critical chapter in the 2014 Fifth Assessment Report of the Intergovernmental Panel on Climate Change (AR5) employ tuning, the word "tuning" appears there only fourteen times. That number includes once in the table of contents and once in the reference list. Of the chapter's 1,423 references, only one contains the word "tuning" in its title! Contrast that with the number of appearances in that chapter of the word "cloud" or "clouds" (165), "aerosol" (120), "ice" (333), and "ocean" or "oceans" (638). Although AR6 was not yet complete at the time of this writing, neither the word "model" or "models" nor the word "tuning" appears in the title of any of the report's twelve listed chapters.

Interpreting such information to be indicative of a deliberate lack of transparency, a 2017 article by fifteen climatologists ascribes it to an uneasiness within the climatology community over its use of tuning, especially since twenty-two of the twenty-three modeling centers contacted in a survey reported in the article said their models had used tuning while all responded that they believed tuning to be important in model development. Climatologists evidently have two minds about tuning.

According to that article, its title being "The Art and Science of Climate Model Tuning," the practice of tuning is partly subjective and partly objective. Uneasy about the subjective part, the article's authors cite as authoritative support for the use of tuning a 1922 article by the highly respected statistician R. A. Fisher identifying "parameter estimation" as one of three steps comprising the process of model development. As noted earlier, to those authors, but not to Fisher, parameter estimation meant the partially subjective process of estimating influence values ("independent variables" to statisticians). To Fisher, it meant an entirely objective process of estimating the weights in a weighted sum of influence values, commonly to minimize error variation. So the citation of Fisher was hardly authoritative support for the subjective part of tuning. To the extent that subjectivity plays a part in it, climatologists have every reason to be uneasy about tuning.

Subjectivity-objectivity, however, is not the correct scale to use in evaluating the practice of tuning. As indicated later, the correct scale to use is the right-wrong one, and on this scale, regardless of the extent of subjectivity or objectivity involved in the practice, tuning is simply wrong. "Parameters" as the term is used by both hydrogeologists and climatologists are data, and Fisher was not endorsing the adjustment of data.

Simply the alteration of an influence value itself does not constitute tuning. An alteration made to use a model to predict a future event when the influence values may differ from their current values is not tuning. The difference is that in tuning, the observations being predicted, from past to present, remain unchanged throughout the process whereas in prediction of the future, those observations are free to vary, as are the influence values.

One last item of interest in the comparison of "parameter" adjustment in hydrogeology and climatology: whereas the hydrogeologists cited in my *Chance* article blamed their calibrated models for being too slow to catch up with the data, climatologists have tended to blame the data for being too slow to catch up with their tuned models. Neither the models nor the data are to blame, however. The blame belongs entirely to the practice of calibration or tuning itself.

By exaggerating upward or downward trends of observations over time, tuning corrupts data. When it is done to improve the appearance of a model or to help produce desired model results, it descends to the level of cheating. It is like using a cheat sheet to answer questions you would otherwise get wrong on a test. On the binary scale of right and wrong, regardless of the motivation, it is simply wrong.

A mindset that allows tuning to help a model achieve a desired purpose can allow not only its extreme use but also the use of other forms of such motivated data manipulation. In chapter 4 of *Unsettled*, Koonin cites a glaring example. Global warming being a United Nations' concern, the models described in figure 2 come from countries all over the world. To correct for a prediction of over twice as much global warming as was observed, some highly regarded German climatologists tuned one of their independent variables (influence values) by a factor of ten from its initial value in their model-improvement process. Not to be outdone, a hydrogeologist cited in my *Chance* article adjusted an influence value to be orders of magnitude larger on one side than on the other side of a river crossing an aquifer below it to show that the aquifer was not getting any of its water from the river above it. To achieve a sensitivity of 3.0°C for CO_2 concentration, a modeler could avoid tuning altogether simply by fixing the sensitivity for CO_2 concentration at 3.0°C while allowing data to determine the sensitivities for the other influence values in model development. Such blatant fudging of results should sound an alarm in every research community, not only climatology, to avoid the practice of data manipulation by any means to help achieve a desired purpose.

In addition to the steep rise in mean global warming from about 1970 onward, figure 2 also shows an equally steep rise earlier, between about 1900 and 1940, prior to the steep rise in the use of fossil fuels. As shown by the gray swath in the figure, however, the model predictions rise about twice as steeply for the later than for the earlier period, a difference noted with concern by Koonin in *Unsettled*. Koonin feared that the models were not sensitive enough to natural conditions, like a burst of unrecorded volcanic activity beneath the sea (my, not Koonin's, example), causing the earlier rise that might also, possibly—though not necessarily—together with CO_2, be the cause of the later rise. Tuning might also help explain the difference.

Prior to tuning, the model predictions tracked the observations with mostly randomly occurring under- and over predictions. That tendency applied to both the earlier and the later periods of steep observation rise, but only during the later period did the measured concentration of CO_2 rise precipitously. So, prior to tuning, the models could better, likely much better, account for the rise in that later period than for the rise in the earlier period. By exaggerating both rises, tuning improved the performance appearance of the models during the earlier period while having the opposite effect during the later period of steep observation rise.

The United Nations' studies of global warming have employed enormous resources involving the use of many computers working in concert for months to analyze data from all the defined zones above the surface of the land and below the surface of the oceans throughout the world. Because of the enormity of the undertaking, much of the data collected is either unreliable or just an expert guess, a condition that invites and may, in some minds, even justify tuning. Some hydrogeologists who are aware of the problems resulting from their calibration of a model have in each instance resolved them by developing a new model based on the adjusted data in the calibrated one. Climatologists have done likewise, now in their sixth iteration (AR6), with increasingly unsatisfactory results motivating more rather than less tuning and showing increased divergence among modelers from iteration to iteration, duly noted by Koonin in *Unsettled*.

Perhaps in an excess of hutzpah, a statistician who is not a climatologist might offer the following possible solution to the tuning problem in climatology: Analyze the data obtained from a random sample of zones that is large enough to yield results having an acceptable margin of error and small enough for researchers to collect reliable data from all the zones in the sample. A small number of climatologists have already begun to do that. Rather than being an exception, random sampling should become the norm.

The number of zones needed to do that would be in the low thousands rather than the millions now under study.

The planet is going through an interglacial period of global warming. Carbon dioxide fills little holes in the blanket of water vapor in the sky that helps keep the earth warm. Human activity that varies the production of CO_2 may somewhat affect the rate but cannot stop the occurrence of global warming. Despite what the cock might believe, the sun will continue to rise even if he stops crowing before daybreak. Guided by research in climatology, with due respect for Mother Nature, human beings in this century should plan for steadily rising seas resulting from melting glaciers and icebergs—along with other daunting challenges—created by increasingly warm nights. The name of the effort could be Project Noah. It has happened before.

This is where the article ended. That was about a year and a half ago. In the article, as well as this chapter so far, I have attempted to be as accurate and objective as possible to meet the standards of a scientific journal. For some readers, the objectivity may seem, perhaps unnecessarily, to have been excessive. That is no longer a constraint for me now. Even so, in reworking the article for this chapter, I did not want to write as an expert expecting readers to believe my conclusions without having to understand them on their own. That is why my explanations may have seemed more than a bit laborious. If so, that was likely due to my attempt to keep the mathematics required for understanding my explanations no more challenging than eighth grade arithmetic. I avoided calculus, algebra, and even multiplication and division. So I have no apologies to readers who may have found my explanations, particularly near the beginning of the chapter, too tedious to read further. On the contrary, I applaud you readers who plowed through and got as far as these final pages, where I now feel free to speak my mind.

To date, though the article appeared in a journal having a name forbidding to anyone who is not a statistician, 419 people have signed up to read it, 80 of them to make copies of it. Many of them may be climatologists, to some of whom I sent the article. Readers of this chapter should realize that the article came out too late to influence the 2023 Sixth Assessment Report of the Intergovernmental Panel on Climate Change (AR6), which was nearing completion as I was completing work on the article. That recent report unfortunately remains the basis of arguments made for erroneously attributing most, if even any, of the cause of global warming to human activity. My hope now is that after having access to the information provided here, people who made that mistake would change their minds and their behavior, most of which has been based on a widely held and deeply entrenched belief that human existence—perhaps due to our free will or, in some minds, to original sin—is an existential threat to the rest of the world. Somehow, if we are to survive as a species, let alone as a country, we are going to have to get over that.

CHAPTER 6

The 2020 Presidential Election

The 2020 Presidential Election: **What Went Wrong?**

Each State shall appoint, <u>in such Manner as the Legislature thereof may direct</u>, a Number of Electors, equal to the whole Number of Senators and Representatives to which the State may be entitled in the Congress.

—"Article II: Section 1"

"The 2020 presidential election was free and fair" and "Donald Trump lied when he claimed that Joe Biden's win was unlawful" are both incorrect statements, contrary to the expressed and implied opinions of the legacy media, meaning most media other than Fox. I invite anyone who thinks or believes otherwise to read on. The second statement is a good place to start if for no reason other than the almost ubiquitous though erroneous use of the word "lie" when referring to Trump's belief about the conduct of that election.

My claim here is not that Democrats committed consequential fraud in the counting of votes cast in Democrat-run states. No one can doubt that some fraud in vote counting did occur, but postelection studies have shown that the amount of that fraud was too little to have influenced the election's outcome. In other words, fraud did occur, but its occurrence was inconsequential. That is where most of the media end their inquiry and conclude that the election results were lawful without question.

Without question? No, the question is huge, and Trump has every reason to believe that, even without vote-counting fraud, the election was anything but lawful. The best place to start addressing that issue is the legal case brought by Texas Attorney General Ken Paxton on December 8, 2020, in State of Texas versus Commonwealth of Pennsylvania, State of Georgia, State of Michigan, and State of Wisconsin (*Texas v. Pennsylvania et al.*, for short) and denied by the Supreme Court on December 11, 2020, briefly as follows: "Texas lacks 'Article III' standing to sue other states over how they conduct their own elections. Case dismissed."

Like almost all the other legal actions questioning the legality of the election, this one ended on a procedural issue, without considering it on the arguments and evidence presented by the plaintiff. What were those arguments and that evidence in this case? They were simply that the four defendant states failed to follow the United States Constitution, specifically "Article II: Section 1: Clause 2," focused on the excerpt at the beginning of this chapter: "Each State shall appoint, in such Manner as the Legislature thereof may direct, a Number of Electors, equal to the whole Number of Senators and Representatives to which the State may be entitled in the Congress" ("Article II: Section 1"; underlining mine).

What did those four states do wrong? Here is what Pennsylvania did wrong: Failing to follow the requirement of its commonwealth constitution that, with limited exceptions, a person vote only on Election Day, a commonwealth court in December 1919 legalized no- excuse mail-in balloting and extended the mailing date to three days following Election Day. Changing the constitutional requirement lawfully would have required an amendment to the state constitution, not simply an action by a state court. The unlawful change made by a court in Pennsylvania was consequential: The commonwealth lost track of more ballots than the difference in votes between Trump and Biden.

Although Georgia law prohibits the counting of mail-in ballots prior to the morning of Election Day, the state election board, not the legislature, allowed processing of ballots up to three weeks before Election Day. That was a clear violation of the United States Constitution. How that change could have affected the election outcome may not be obvious. Still, the reason it was made is no less obvious and, for that reason, makes it suspicious, as well as unlawful.

Although Michigan state law requires that voters make individual, formal, signed applications for absentee ballots, the state's secretary of state set up a website for them to obtain their absentee ballots. Michigan's secretary of state is not its legislature, and so Michigan's election procedure was also in violation of the United States Constitution. What effect that violation may have had on the state's election results may or may not be consequential, but still it was an unlawful action. A bank robber who is caught with his haul in his hands does not walk away free of charge. Neither should Michigan.

Wisconsin state law prohibits the use of unmanned drop boxes for ballots, but the state's elections commission and others, excluding its legislature, permitted the use of hundreds of drop boxes, many of them unmanned, in clear violation of the United States Constitution. That was no less than ballot-harvesting heaven.

One hundred and twenty-six members of Congress supported the Texas case, as did seventeen other states, in *amicus* briefs. The case was denied summarily, but its complaint was not a whistle in the wind. If no state had standing to make the complaint, then the action to take is not simply to forget about it but to determine who does have standing and try to get that who to do it.

That is precisely what President Trump did when he asked, even implored, Mike Pence to carry out his oath as vice president when on January 6, 2021, he as president of the Senate led the joint session of Congress to receive all the electoral college votes and, based on the total of their count for each candidate, to determine and announce officially who the next president of the United States would be. Vice President Mike Pence chose to do otherwise.

What could and what should he have done? He, like all others who have held his office, took the following oath of office: "I do solemnly swear [or affirm] that I will faithfully execute the Office of Vice President of the United States, and will to the best of my Ability, preserve, protect and defend the Constitution of the United States" (my underlining). Pence has claimed that this oath is what prompted him to do what he did and not what his president had asked him to do. What did Pence do? He simply accepted all the votes presented by the states without question, but where in the Constitution does it say that his role, as he has claimed many times, was only ceremonial? In fact, his role was more, much more, than that. It was, following his oath as underlined above, to "preserve, protect and defend the Constitution of the United States."

What does that mean in this case? What else could it mean but to ask each representative presenting a voting result to say under oath, under penalty of perjury, that the vote was taken in accordance with the requirements set forth in "Article II: Section 1: Clause 2" of the United States Constitution? Representatives of at least four of the states, the ones cited specifically in this chapter, could not have truthfully said yes. In that event, the vice president, following his oath, would have to have had to disqualify the votes of those four states. What recourse would those states have had then? Their only recourse would have been to present their case to the United States Supreme Court, where *they,* as injured parties, would have had standing. As that court did in the 2000 Gore versus Bush election, it would, in this case, have had to require, prior to the January 20, 2021, date of the inauguration, a vote from each of the four delinquent states that this time conformed with the requirements of "Article II: Section 1: Clause 2" of the Constitution.

Otherwise, the vote of any of the four states that failed to comply with that order would not have counted or, more precisely, would have counted as zero for any candidate. What would have happened in the likely case that none of the four defendant states could come up with a constitutionally valid vote? The answer to that question is the very reason Texas filed *Texas v. Pennsylvania et al.* Biden's 305 of the total 538 electoral college votes cast would have been reduced by the 62 constitutionally uncountable votes of the four delinquent states to 243 while Trump would have retained his 232 votes. Neither would have had the majority of 270 (one more than half of the total 538) votes required to win the election. In that case, the Constitution in "Article II: Section 1: Clause 3" requires that the House of Representatives make the choice, the representatives for each state having only one vote. Since the number of red states exceeded the number of blue states in the House prior to January 6, 2020, the choice of that chamber would likely have been Trump, not Biden.

These observations are not just an exercise in logic for the sake of argument. State courts in two of the four defendant states ruled against the unconstitutional changes in their 2020 voting procedures, in Michigan by a single judge on March 16, 2021, and in Wisconsin by its supreme court on July 8, 2022, in a 4–3 vote.

So Trump was not wrong to believe that he lawfully would have won the 2020 presidential election, and having that belief, he certainly was not lying when he expressed it.

Trump was not the villain. The Democrats in the four delinquent states who unconstitutionally changed the voting rules there were certainly villains, but even they do not account for all the wrongdoing. Vice President Pense is guilty too. The wrongdoers in the four states used the pandemic as an excuse for their misbehavior. That excuse was no better than the excuse of four children who stayed home from school because it was raining when the rest of the class managed to make it through the rain. Pense's excuse was equally poor. His interpretation of his oath of office, that it restricted him simply to accept the count of votes as presented on January 6, 2021, without even considering objections from members of Congress as though they were just decorations in attendance at a ceremonial event, is 180 degrees in the wrong direction from the requirement of his oath that he, having sole responsibility on that date, ensure that the votes presented by the states were obtained in accordance with the Constitution.

What the vice president did was even worse than that. His disclosure a day earlier of what he planned to do on January 6, 2021, was the direct cause of the protest march that got out of hand by people who strongly believed that Pence's job was to expose rather than to hide possibly existing and consequential flaws of the election. What Pence did instead with his announcement of his intention the day before was to motivate the Oath Keepers and the Proud Boys to carry out their contingency plans to foment an assault on the Capitol. Pence, no less than House Speaker Nancy Pelosi in her turning down President Trump's offer of thousands of national guard personnel to protect the Capitol, was responsible for the assault.

Trump and the Oath Keepers and the Proud Boys and the marchers on the Capitol were not the only people who smelled a rat in the 2020 election. Over seventy million voters, including me, who is not even a Republican, believed the election was anything but free and fair, as claimed by most Democrats.

Trump's lying about the election being itself a lie, so how about the election's being free and fair?

Freedom either includes freedom from censorship or the First Amendment to the Constitution has no meaning. Having possessed Hunter Biden's notorious laptop since December 2019, what was the Federal Bureau of Investigation doing on October 14, 2020, just hours before the *New York Post* publication of its story about Hunter Biden's notorious laptop when a team of its agents began to request the major social media to censor all information about the laptop, particularly its disclosure of Hunter's sale of access to his vice president father for millions of dollars paid by devious means to members of his family, including his father? What the FBI was doing was influencing the 2020 election in favor of Joe Biden and breaking the Constitution to do it. In fact, surveys have shown that, if, prior to the election, voters had known about the existence and contents of the laptop, enough of them would have switched their vote from Biden to Trump to change the results of the election.

So much for the 2020 election's being free; now how about its being fair?

Was it fair that fifty-one former federal government intelligence officials on October 19, 2020, two weeks before the November 3 election, signed a letter deceptively claiming that the Hunter Biden laptop story had all the earmarks of Russian propaganda, a letter that, in a critical television debate with Trump, Biden cited to support his claim that the story about his son and the laptop was pure "garbage"? No, it was not fair unless being fair includes being deceitful.

So how did all this lawbreaking and deceit work out for the Democrats? It worked out rather well, of course. The Democrats won the election. They beat the Republicans, but that is not the end of this story. What is important to realize about the Democrats is that in their minds, the Republicans are no longer their true enemy. Their true enemy, at least since the beginning of the current administration, has been Christianity, most pointedly the Catholic Church, which has dominated Western civilization for almost two thousand years. Many, perhaps the majority, of elected Democrats and others now believe that civilization has advanced far beyond the time when it should have openly acknowledged its realization that Christianity is based on the false promise that people can live forever if only they publicly embrace the truth of a highly unreasonable story. Although those Democrats consider anyone who believes otherwise to be pathetically naive, they fail to see the irony of their own false promise of utopia for people who follow them along the socialist path away from religion. No one has ever returned from a socialist utopia to confirm that it exists just as no one has ever returned from a Christian heaven to confirm its existence.

Be that as it may, Christianity has been the enemy of socialism for a long time in places where the Republican party does not even exist. Christianity is the enemy of socialism simply because Christianity has had the power that socialism seeks. Even democracy is not the enemy of socialism. Europe is full of democratic socialist parties and has been at least as long ago as Hitler's National Socialist Party. China holds elections in what it calls a socialist consultative democracy, which is a Republican-like hierarchical democracy.

Democracy is not the enemy of socialism. Its enemy is religion in general and particularly Christianity and—even more so—the Catholic Church, where the power in Western civilization has been for centuries, as shown by the crosses on so many flags in Europe. Socialism worldwide is the modern replacement of religion. No doubt the most consequential issue dividing the two sides is abortion, which could alone account for the difference between winners and losers in elections.

The dominating religion in the Republican Party is Catholicism, which unequivocally opposes abortion at any stage of pregnancy. Republican protestants also tend to be more religiously observant than their

Democrat counterparts, who have increasingly been becoming socialist agnostics over at least the past decade. The difference between winners and losers in the swing states has been so small that winning over even miniscule portions of the population can make the difference between winners and losers. That is probably the dominant reason Democrats have wooed the 7.2 percent of LBGTQ in the nation's population over to their side. Democrats have also counted on larger demographic groups like Black and Hispanic people at least since President Johnson's Great Society legislation. Donald Trump's success in winning over a portion of each of those two groups in the 2016 and 2020 elections is a significant reason Democrats have opposed him so unmercifully since he won the 2016 election.

Both unfree and unfair is the endemic and unabashed censoring and lying of the modern legacy media, which affect not just small portions of the population but virtually the entire population. A good question to ask now is, How did so many journalists fall so low? This is where academia comes in.

When I began college in 1948, the faculty were predominantly Republicans, so much so that when I organized a caravan to drive to the San Francisco Cow Palace in 1952 to attend a rally by Humphrey Bogart and Lauren Bacall for Adlai Stevenson, I was the only student, together with a single faculty member, who made up the caravan. That one faculty member, more than just interestingly, turned out to be special in other ways as well. Though at least ostensibly a Democrat, he later became a department chairman, a dean of humanities and sciences, and a president of the American Psychological Association, as well as my favorite faculty member in my over five years at Stanford. So political affiliations at universities began to change even as early as I left college to join the Army during the Korean conflict in the early 1950s.

How did they change? The increasing number of exchange students since World War II, which sharpened American awareness of Europe and Asia, certainly bolstered the change, which may have begun with the growing realization among academics—who, following World War II, were perhaps, for the first time, teaching students who would not have attended college without the GI Bill— that college was not only for the elite. That was a valid realization then, but unfortunately, now it has devolved into an erroneous belief that college is for everyone, regardless of promise.

Contributing to that unfortunate devolution, no doubt, was the advent of the federal student loan. The availability of that loan made it literally possible for virtually anyone, including a prospective journalist, to attend college, and virtually everyone so inclined has been doing so and thereby enabling colleges to raise tuition and faculty pay yearly far beyond the rate of inflation.

At the same time as American students through the exchange program were becoming increasingly aware of European culture, particularly in universities, so were American faculty members. Perhaps astonishing to both was the extremely high esteem professors had in Europe in sharp contrast to the United States. That astonishment could well have grown into academia's current love of European culture, including its left-sided politics. The result, along with a growing far-left opposition to traditional morality in universities and an increasing but unearned self-esteem of faculty members accompanying their increasing pay and identification with their European counterparts, has been lower college admissions standards, less challenging academic courses and requirements for graduation, and graduates having inadequate skills for the work they thought their degree would entitle them, along with having the weighty obligation under those circumstances of having to pay off their student loans. Stanford is no longer the school it was when I was there. Nor is Princeton, where I completed my graduate work after getting out of the Army. Both now have replaced the straight and narrow with a broad and costly path to nowhere.

Aside from the assent of socialism and the decline of religion, both changes I abhor, I say that now not as a member of the elite, fearful of dislodgment—for them, things are never so good as they used to be—but as a person who long ago lived in a country that gave him the opportunity to work his way through costly but demanding colleges with aid by scholarships, fellowships, and the GI Bill. Oh, how I wish that country could come back!

As for the election in 2020, alarmed and disheartened by all the unfree and unfair shenanigans the Democrats used to win it, oh, how I wish for the 2024 return of the 2016 election result!

CHAPTER 7

Joseph Robinette Biden Jr.

Joseph Robinette Biden Jr.: **Wheeling and Dealing**

Here's the deal.

—JRB Jr.

Though the most apt ones I could find, "flabbergasted" and "dumbfounded" are strong adjectives that are far from being strong enough to describe how I felt when I learned that Joe Biden had won the 2020 presidential election. Flabbergasted because I was sick to my stomach about the future of our county and dumbfounded because I just could not believe it. This chapter tells why with an eye on the future.

Originally, my plan was to end this book with a chapter on the 2024 election, but things and my thinking about them have changed since I began writing. The most influential change is that it now seems much less likely than it did several months ago that Biden will be the nominee of his party. Although I had expected that under Biden the country would go in the opposite direction of heaven in a handbasket full of Hillary Clinton's "deplorables" who voted against her in 2016 and for him in 2020, things had become so much worse than I had anticipated that even the Democrats have been coming to believe that Biden had to go. What I came to realize is that my intent had been not to write about the upcoming election so much as to write about Biden himself, as well as my feelings and opinions about him that are likely shared by the tens of millions of my companions in Hillary's basket.

To help explain my flabbergasted and dumfounded feelings about the 2020 election result, a good place to begin is to tell how I came to be an occupant of that basket. In 2016, when Hillary was opposing Donald Trump in the election for the presidency, I was a

Democrat, as I had been since birth eighty-six years earlier. Hillary's bald-faced, self-aggrandizing prevarication in public had annoyed me so much that I just could not vote for her. My wife, who had been a lifetime Republican, suggested that, horror of horrors, I watch the Fox News Network, particularly the show by Sean Hannity, which we had started watching together when it began in 1996 with conservative Hannity and liberal Alan Colmes as cohosts. When Colmes left the show in 2008, I stopped watching it. Watching Hannity again in 2016 softened my opposition to the Republican Party enough so when Hillary, in a campaign speech, identified half of the people who opposed her as members of a basket of deplorables, I immediately identified myself as a charter member of that basket and, as such, cast my vote for Donald Trump, bolstered by my rationalization that, unlike Hillary, he was a billionaire who could not be bought.

Once Trump was in office, I became increasingly happy about my voting choice. The major things he promised to do while campaigning he, in fact, did while in office. Control the border? Check. Get rid of ISIS? Check. Leave Social Security alone? Check. End the Iran nuclear deal and intensify sanctions against the country? Check. Replace the Canada-Mexico trade agreement with one much better for us? Check. Impose tariffs on China to balance the lopsided cash flow between our two countries? Check. Cut taxes? Double check. With that record and a superb economy and with no war raging in the world around us, what more could we want in a president? And, whatever that what more might have been, how in the real world could we have expected Joe Biden, who had one of the Senate's most lackluster records of accomplishment, to do it? His win in 2020 just made no sense at all to me, at least with all else being equal.

So my conclusion, shared by tens of millions of others, is that all else could not have been equal. The previous chapter went into the details of that and demonstrated that, in fact, all else was far from equal. The print, the television, and the online media were not equal. The justice department and the Federal Bureau of Investigation were not equal. Academia, big business, and the entertainment media were not equal. All were biased against Trump. Instead of addressing that bias with arguments and evidence, the courts, including the Supreme Court, tragically buried it in a procedural grave. That is why I was flabbergasted.

So now why was I dumbfounded? That is an especially good adjective to describe my feelings though not nearly their intensity. I just could not believe after four years of a president who had brought us peace and prosperity that so many Americans could be dumb enough to vote against him for a person having such a mediocre political record as Biden. How, after Trump had done just about everything he had promised to do, could that have happened? Even harder to understand is how that could have happened just after Trump, in only a matter of months, had developed a vaccine to combat the pandemic, a vaccine that ordinarily would have taken several years to develop. Where were the appreciation and the gratitude and the common sense?

While Trump campaigned in numerous rallies attended by tens of thousands of people, Biden mostly remained in the basement of his home and, when he did go out to campaign, faced only tiny audiences of people confined to their automobiles, his excuse being fear of catching and spreading the pandemic virus. Shared with tens of millions of others under those circumstances, my shock by the election result was so severe that it approached the level of the shock (though certainly not the anguish) experienced in Israel by the Hamas's surprise attack on October 7, 2023. That is because both events were earthshaking to the extent of their being revolutionary in their threats to turn our two worlds upside down. The difference is that Israel can fight back while our hands here in America have been tied by our

Constitution, the only fight we have been able to muster being the pathetically ineffective occupation of the Capitol on January 6, 2021.

So much about me and my basket companions. Now about Biden, the star of this chapter. As an adolescent exercise, finding words to describe Biden is easy. All you must do is list the words the print media use in their opinion columns, letters to the editor, and news stories to describe Donald Trump.

Narcissist. Who has had hair transplants and facial surgery to improve his appearance and dresses like a model wearing mafioso shades? Not Trump, but certainly Biden fits the bill.

Liar. Who, when on television, lies to people straight in their faces when he tells false stories about himself involving business with his son Hunter or meetings with Nelson Mandela and Golda Meir or fires in his kitchen or his being at the top of his class in law school when, in fact, he was at the bottom? The list is so long that it trumps Trump's even as composed by Democrats.

Plagiarist. Who has given speeches written and made by others as if they were his own? Answer: Biden, not

Trump.

Arrogant. Again, Biden wins mainly because his achievements supporting an attitude of superiority pale in contrast to Trump's.

Ignorant. Of the two men, Biden—if we are, in actuality, talking about a lack of common sense—certainly deserves that distinction.

Racist. No contest. Biden wins hands down. Who was the one who said integrated schools would be "racial jungles" or Republicans "are going to put y'all back in chains" or "if you don't vote for me, you ain't Black"?

Incompetent. During the term of which man did our country have peace and prosperity and during the term of which man did it have neither? Your answers to those two questions tell which man is the less competent of the two.

Idiot. As an expert on mental testing, I say without equivocation that Biden wins this epithet by a country mile. Trump is a genius by contrast. Here we must realize again that all these epithets are adolescent, if not childish, and this one the most childish of all. Of course, neither Trump nor Biden is an idiot. Expect more on this issue later.

Crooked. Biden would not be where he is if he had not arrived there by hook and by crook. By what achievement other than crime could he have become a multimillionaire? Golf courses and hotels? No, those were Trump's. Whose income taxes have been made public? Same answer, Trump's, not Biden's. Who is trying to win a presidential election by indicting his opponent? You answer that one.

Contrary to some of the others, the issue of crime is not a joke. In an ongoing impeachment inquiry, Congress is investigating Biden for his role in his son Hunter's international pay-for-play business. Although in support of Biden, the legacy media have been almost entirely silent on the investigation's targets, perhaps the most widely known of them is a 2014 Ukrainian quid-pro-quo scheme. The quid in this scheme was that Joe, as vice president, would secure the dismissal of a Ukrainian prosecutor who had been investigating fraud by a Ukrainian energy company that had his son Hunter on its board at over eighty-three thousand dollars a month, and the quo would be that the chairman of that board pay an additional ten million dollars to Biden's family. All those actions occurred. The only question remaining, under investigation by Congress, is the amount of money Joe himself received for his role in the scheme.

Neither is it a joke that, of the two men, Biden and Trump, Biden is the one who is sitting in the Oval Office as our country's captain while the world burns, not from global warming but from global war, and our country burns, not fossil fuel but money, while millions of illegal migrants, including terrorists, pour into our country through its southern border. Let us take a moment now to look at this last issue. I have mostly ignored it in this book up until now because it hardly deserves more than a few words, let alone a chapter, because it is so irrational and indefensible. These words, which were the last paragraph of letter I wrote for the July 26, 2023, edition of the *Monterey Herald*, will suffice:

If President Biden is not getting a substantial cut from the Mexican cartels vastly enriched by the migration he makes possible at our southern border, then he needs an exceptionally strong dose of artificial intelligence to make up for his lack of the real stuff.

This man has over a year remaining in his current term, regardless of whether he runs for another four years. To help us survive now, we need to have a truly deep understanding of him to be able to persuade him to change the course of our ship of state, if possible, as soon as possible.

So now is the time for me to put my psychologist hat on. With that hat firmly on my head, I can now say with some authority that Joseph R. Biden Jr. resembles a bona fide sociopath.

What does it mean to be a sociopath? It means that human beings, who, unlike other animals, are born with only residual instincts that are insufficient to help them survive, must depend on intelligence, particularly judgment, and learned skills to make it through life. Although we do not respond directly to instinctual impulses, most of us feel and recognize their residuals as conscience, the uncomfortable feeling we have when we believe we may have done something wrong. Sociopaths are the exception. They do not have those feelings to help guide them in their behavior. Human beings are social animals who must live together to survive. For most people, the feeling of residual instincts that would naturally have impelled normal social interaction, our conscience, comes when we are beginning to behave unsocially, its function being to help us curb that behavior. Sociopaths must live without that help. They perceive other human beings not as people with whom they can interact but as people they can use to survive or thrive. So, without conscience or embarrassment, they can lie and cheat when they feel that will further their self-interests. They are much more focused on themselves than on others. They view others as simply means to an end. If you see that Biden might fit this bill, then we agree.

That does not mean that Biden is, in fact, a sociopath. More likely, more charitably, and more usefully, it means that he is more flexible in his behavior than someone who is guided more strongly by conscience than by self-interest. His flexibility, in fact, is what, perhaps more than anything else, enabled him not only to survive in politics for more than half a century but also to achieve its highest offices, particularly the current one. Not being committedly far-Right or far-Left or even somewhere in between, he was sufficiently flexible in 2020 to swing far to the Left in a deal with that side of his party. Here's the deal: Instead of opposing Biden, Bernie Sanders would support him as the nominee of their party and would put the highly energetic far-Left side of the party behind him in the election if Biden agreed to implement their Green New Deal platform should he become president. He agreed, they did, and he won.

Now consider Biden's judgment.

Judgment is the highest level of intelligence, and not everyone achieves it. The next lower level is adolescence, and that is as high as Biden has reached, at least in his administration. Evidence? At the adolescent level, a person believes that to become an independent adult, all you must do is do the opposite of what your parents require or set an example for you to do. That is precisely what Biden did when he entered the office of the presidency. He did the very opposite of his predecessor. He turned every policy he inherited from Trump upside down. He reopened the border. He cut fossil fuels. He ended sanctions against Iran. He pulled our troops completely out of Afghanistan while leaving their highly costly air base and arms behind them for the Taliban, who took over. In forming his administration, he threw merit out the window and replaced it with a rainbow of colors. He rejoined our country to the Paris Agreement on climate change while allowing China and India as "developing nations" to continue their burn-baby-burn behavior. This is just a partial list, but it is sufficient to make the point. The Biden administration lacks judgment.

Notice I said the Biden administration, not necessarily Biden himself, lacks judgment. That is because Biden has not made his policy decisions by himself. Obligated by his agreement with Sanders, Biden has made most, if not all, of those decisions as the chairman of a committee whose function is to ensure that all administration decisions support the Green New Deal. That is why I identified Biden in the title of this book as chairman, not as president. That is why this book, except for Chapter 1, never refers to Biden as president. The Biden administration operates like the central committee of the Communist Party of China. For Chairman Biden to become President Biden, he must personally review all his policy decisions to date and use his own common sense, not group think, to reverse the ones that have gotten our country and the world into so much trouble.

Adolescent leadership, without judgment, is dangerous not just for the country but for the entire world. What can we do about it? All *we* can do is try to persuade the occupant of the Oval Office to reverse course. By the way Biden won the election, via a deal, he has shown that he has the flexibility to do that. If he is a true sociopath or even if he just has the flexibility of one, then—with the appropriate quid pro quo—I believe persuasion is worth a serious attempt.

That persuasion should consist of a behind-closed-doors offer of a deal with its quid being what we want Biden to do and its quo being what we are willing to do for him in return. This option seems too shady even to discuss it in public, but we have no other option that has a chance of succeeding for us to avoid further meltdown of our country internally and of its power to deter or control world conflict.

Who could make such a deal? Who else other than the former president and author of the book *The Art of the Deal?* Donald Trump, of course. No one knows how better than he does how to determine the quid and the quo of the deal. The time is quickly becoming ripe to do it. Biden has already begun to change his border policy with a recent decision to build a portion of Trump's planned wall. Biden's recent speeches on the treacherous Hamas incursion into Israel and Iran's culpability in it are also indicative of his possible readiness to change course completely on these and other issues. If the Democrats dump him as their candidate for the 2024 election or even just threaten to do so, then Biden should be ripe for the deal. The Biden administration is almost three years old. It is more than time for it to grow up.

Before ending this book, I must say how I came to write it. Like most other Jews of my age, I was born a Democrat. For reasons I explained earlier, that changed in 2016. I could not become a Republican because the 30 or 40 percent of them are RINOs whom I view as political descendants of the Republicans who kept Jews out of country clubs. I also could not become a Libertarian because they believe the correlation between age and wisdom is much higher than I do. So, instead, together with my wife who had been a Republican, I became an Independent, on the conservative side, because that isthe side I was on when I had been a Democrat. Accompanying my transition, as noted earlier, I became a supporter of Donald Trump, an increasingly ardent supporter as his presidency went on because of his accomplishments.

One of the main reasons I am writing this book is to show the gross mischaracterization of Trump supporters as occupants of Hillary's basket of deplorables who are "racist, sexist, homophobic, xenophobic, Islamophobic," or, more succinctly and arguably in former President Barack Obama's words, "cling to guns or religion or antipathy to people who aren't like them." Hillary's mischaracterizations are just plain puerile and unfounded name- calling unworthy of further comment. If Barack's were correct, how could I be an occupant of Hillary's basket? As a Jew, I am certainly not a Tea Party member though I highly respect its membership. I support gun ownership not because I am crazy about guns but because I support the Second Amendment as, in its words, "necessary to the security of a free state." Far from being a high school dropout, also included in the negative stereotype of a basket occupant, I have three college degrees, including a PhD. What we, occupants of Hillary's basket, have in common, in addition to a deep love of our country, is respectful and appreciative support of Donald Trump. Here, only partially, is why:

He has character. Unlike most adults, he neither smokes nor drinks. He keeps his word.

He is hardworking. When president, he worked almost every day of the week and far into the night. Contrast that with Biden's work record in office, 40 percent of his time on vacation and an early "cap" on his workday, sometimes even before noon.

He has sound judgment, unimpaired by an unhealthful lifestyle.

He is unflaggingly confrontational with forces inside and outside our country who oppose his efforts to "make America great again," his MAGA.

His weapons of choice are words and dollars rather than bullets and bombs, but he is not reluctant to use bullets or bombs, when necessary, as in the cases of Soleimani and Baghdadi. With bullets and bombs, he chooses his targets carefully.

Being a highly successful businessman and having a master's degree in business administration, he understands capitalism and the freedom of competition it depends upon.

He believes in the equality of opportunity rather than the equity of outcome.

He is not a racist. Along with Martin Luther King, he believes in the evaluation of people not by the color of their skin but by the content of their character.

He believes in a meritocracy, based on skill, not a mediocracy, based on identity.

He relates well with people at all economic and educational levels of society and with every ethnicity. He is the father of the Abraham Accords, bringing Jews and Muslims together.

Although this list is not complete, it is sufficient to show why Donald Trump has such ardent support by the MAGA crowd in Hillary's basket.

To end this chapter and the book, a fitting topic for me, at least, is a discussion of the future of a Democratic Party in our country. The use of "a" instead if "the" in the preceding sentence was, of course, intentional. The Democratic Party I knew for much of my life no longer exists. It has been replaced by a party whose leaders are seeking to emulate, not eliminate, the one led by Chairman Xi Jinping in

China. Unless the current party of Democrats changes course, the identification of the person who occupies the Oval Office will, to me, appropriately remain Chairman Biden.

Realizing that people may differ in their ideas of what that change should be, I am taking my opportunity here to offer my ideas.

Since economics and federalism are properly and traditionally concerns of the Republican Party, the New Democratic Party should restrict its concern with work to union protection of workers outside of government, where the forces of competition operate, and otherwise concentrate on life outside of work, namely culture— art and science—and the environment. Devoid of uniformly strong competitive forces, our whole health system from education and training to research and the delivery of services needs serious bipartisan work, as does our national defense system. Both parties should allow sports and other recreation to flourish naturally, with minimal involvement of politics. Democrats who want to emulate European countries should do it in the cultural areas where those countries have excelled for centuries, not in areas where they have been less successful than we have been, like capitalism and federalism. Our country needs a party with such a mission. Leave experiments with socialism and communism to other countries.

One more thing: be happy to have God bless America.

EPILOGUE

The election is over, and Donald John Trump has won in a landslide, as I predicted in my October 15 interview by Logan Crawford on Spotlight Television -- with 312 Electoral College votes out of a total of 538 and almost five million more popular votes than his competitor, Vice President Kamala Harris. I could not be happier now as a member of Hillary Clinton's Basket of Deplorables. For we are the We of "We the People" who created the Constitution and make sure, with God as our witness and guide, that it will forever remain as the law of our land.

www.ingramcontent.com/pod-product-compliance
Lightning Source LLC
Chambersburg PA
CBHW050003040726
47599CB00014B/1200